CHINESE TRADITIONAL CULTURE SERIES
【中国传统文化精粹书系】

Laws Divine and Human and Pictures of Deities

道德经与神仙画

（英汉对照）

CHINA INTERCONTINENTAL PRESS

五洲传播出版社

Contents

目 录

Preface

Laozi (571-472 BC), the author of Daode Jing, is a philosopher in Spring and Autumn period and the founder of Daoist school. According to the biography of *The Record of the Great Historian*, Laozi surnames Li, first names Er and styles Dan. Some Daoist books take Dan as his posthumous name and Boyang as his honorific name. Some scholar say Lao is his family name, Dan is his first name and his honorific name is Boyang. He was born in some place close to Luyi County, Henan Province. His official position in Zhou's court is on the duty of both the imperial library and archive bureau. Laozi departed from Zhou when he witnessed the elapse of imperial power. It is said that he left the five- thousand-word book which latterly named after him at the request of the pass keeper Yin Xi at Hangu Pass where leads to the Silk Road.

In *Daode Jing*, Laozi established a philosophy centered on Dao. He refers Dao as the extraordinary Way, which transcends but indwells everything. Dao is the origin of the world and Dao is preexistent. "The Dao gives birth to the one, and the one gives birth to the two, the two gives birth to the three, and three gives birth to the myriad of things." Related to Dao, De is the manifestations and realizations of Dao in the world including the humans.

Laozi presents his thought in a style of dialectics, he tends to articulate Dao in twin categories, for example, the beauty and ugliness, blessing and disaster, softness and hardness, yin and yang, etc. His principles, including respect of nature, striving for inner purity, and reduction of personal desire, have been important idealistic goals for Chinese people for tens of centuries.

After the religious tradition was introduced at the turn between the first and the second century, Laozi has been venerated as the Lord, and Daode Jing has been canonized and theologically expounded as the most important sutra.

Daode Jing has been reprinted and commented for formidable times in China. Furthermore, it has been translated most widely only second to the Bible in the modern world. It is taking up its influence on the globe today.

This bi-linguistic version of Daode Jing is illustrated with a lot of ancient paintings and murals which either are related to the ideas of Dao or are directly the descriptions of the immortals. This is our special offerings with this book. In this way, we hope we can share the aesthetical senses, enhance the enlightenment, and increase the reading fun of Daode Jing.

Let us join the pure, silent, natural, ethereal and beautiful tour of Daode Jing.

Wang Yi'e

序

《道德经》的作者老子（约公元前571——前472年），为春秋时期的哲学家，道家学派的创始人。据《史记·老子传》称老子"姓李氏，名耳，字聃"。道书中称"老子姓李，名耳，字伯阳，谥曰聃"；学术界或谓其"姓老，名聃，字伯阳"，楚国苦县（今河南省鹿邑东）厉乡曲仁里人，任周王朝守藏史，是个掌管王室藏书的小官吏。春秋末期，老子见天下战乱频繁，周王室衰败，遂别周而去。相传老子西游，过函谷关，应关令尹喜的请求，为其撰写了《道德经》五千文。

老子在《道德经》中建立了以"道"作为最高范畴的哲学思想体系。老子提出的"道"是"非常道"，即超越常规常识的"道"。老子认为宇宙万物均起源于"道"。"道"具有自然无为，无形无名，不可言说的特性；它还是宇宙万物生成之前的混沌的初始阶段。《道德经》说的"道生一，一生二，二生三，三生万物。万物负阴而抱阳，冲气以为和。"则是宇宙生成演化的最高的自然法则。在《道德经》中，与"道"相对应的是"德"。"德"就是对"道"的体验和认识，即是得道。

在老子的思想中还包含有辩证法的因素，例如对美与丑、祸和福、柔弱与刚强、阴与阳等相互对立又相互依存关系的论述。他所主张的天道自然、清静无为、反朴归真、无为而无不为等思想对中国古代传统哲学以及社会生活的各个方面均有极为深远的影响。《道德经》中的许多哲理和内容，已化作中华民族做人行事的准则，其中的审美思想也成为书画家们的理念和题材。

道教创立后，将老子尊为教祖，将《道德经》奉为自己的重要经典，并对其作出了独特的宗教解释。

《道德经》一书在中国从古到今发行过许多版本，并有许多大家为其作注。近代以来，《道德经》又被翻译成多种文字，在世界各地发行，其发行量仅次于《圣经》，可见其在世界文化史上的地位与影响。

在这本中英文对照的《道德经》中，选用了中国古代多位著名书画家绘制的与老子"道"的思想有关的书画作品和历代描述道教神仙信仰的神仙画。这些书画的选用是这本《道德经》与其它同类书籍不同之处，不仅让人们了解了老子的审美思想，也反映了平面媒体已进入了读图的资讯时代。精美的图文并茂的图书必将丰富与深化着人们对这本千古名著的理解，使人们进一步体悟老子倡导的清静、自然、空灵的境界，让我们在得到文化陶冶的同时又得到了美的享受。

以严肃的哲学经典与美的形式同行，是这本书给读者的最大心愿，我衷心感谢编者们的良苦用心。

王宜峨

Chapter I

The divine law may be spoken of,

but it is not the common law.

Things may be named,

but names are not the things.

In the beginning heaven and earth are

nameless；

when named, all things become known.

So we should be free from desires

in order to understand the internal

mystery of the divine law；

and we should have desires

in order to observe its external

manifestations.

Internal mystery and external

manifestations

come from the same origin,

but have different names,

They may be called essence.

The essential of the essence

is the key to the understanding of all

mysteries.

dì yī zhāng
第 一 章

dào kě dào
道 可 道,

fēi cháng dào
非 常 道;

míng kě míng
名 可 名,

fēi cháng míng
非 常 名。

wú míng tiān dì zhī shǐ
无 名 天 地 之 始;

yǒu míng wàn wù zhī mǔ
有 名 万 物 之 母。

gù cháng wú yù
故 常 无 欲,

yǐ guān qí miào
以 观 其 妙;

cháng yǒu yù
常 有 欲,

yǐ guān qí jiào
以 观 其 徼。

cǐ èr zhě
此 二 者,

tóng chū ér yì míng
同 出 而 异 名,

tóng wèi zhī xuán
同 谓 之 玄。

xuán zhī yòu xuán
玄 之 又 玄,

zhòng miào zhī mén
众 妙 之 门。

Laozi, whose family name is Li, given name is Er, and honorific name is Boyang, was born in Quren Community, Li Town, Ku County, Chu State, in Spring and Autumn period (770~476 BC) His life time was approximately in the 6th century BC. He served as a curator of the dynastic archives records at the court of Zhou. He has mastered the rule of changes from the ancient to modern times. He lived in Zhou for a long time, witnessing the decline of Zhou, he departed on a black ox. When he reached the northwest border, Hangu Pass, separating China from the outside world then, Yin Xi, the official in charge of the border pass, asked that he put his thoughts to writing. The result was a short book consisting of some five thousand Chinese characters. The name "Laozi" is best taken to mean "Old (lao) Master (zi)," and the book has come to be called simply the Laozi. When the Laozi was recognized as a "classic" ("jing" in Chinese) -- that is, a work of such profound insight as to merit canonical status -- it acquired a more exalted and hermeneutically instructive title, the Daodejing (or Tao-Te Ching), commonly translated as the "Classic of the Way and its Virtue." Thereafter, Laozi left; no one knows where he has gone. His influence on Chinese culture is pervasive. Laozi has been regarded as the founder of Daoism which appears as both a school of philosophy (daojia) and a religious tradition (daojiao); in the latter, Laozi is revered as a supreme deity by religious Daoism. Laozi's impact reaches beyond China. Next to the Bible, the Daodejing is the most translated work in world literature today.

老子姓李名耳，字伯阳，春秋(前770—前1476年)时期楚国苦县厉乡曲仁里(今河南省鹿邑县)人，约生活在于公元前6世纪左右，曾做过周朝的守藏史，通晓古今之变，因见周朝衰落，骑青牛离去，在函谷关应尹喜的请求著述五千余言即《道德经》，老子出关后，人们便不知所终。老子思想对中国古代思想文化与宗教的影响非常大，道教便是以老子思想为基础建立起来的，并对现今社会生活的各方面仍有影响意义。

Laozi Riding on an Ox, by Chao Buzhi, Song dynasty

老子骑牛图　晁补之　宋代(960—1279)

Chapter II

If all men in the world know what is fair,

then it is unfair.

If all men know what is good,

then it is not good.

For " to be" and "not to be" co-exist,

There cannot be one without the other:

without "difficult", there cannot be "easy";

without " long", there cannot be "short";

without " high", there cannot be " low";

without sound, there can be no voice；

withou " before", there cannot be "after"；

The contrary complement each other.

Therefore the sage does everything without

interference,

teaches everyone without persuasion,

and lets everything begin uninitiated

and grow unpossessed.

Everything is done without being his deed,

and succeeds without being his success.

Only when success belongs to nobody

does it belong to everyone.

tiān xià   jiē zhī měi zhī wéi měi
天 下 皆 知 美 之 为 美，

sī   è   yǐ
斯 恶 矣；

jiē zhī shàn zhī wéi shàn
皆 知 善 之 为 善，

sī   bù shàn yǐ
斯 不 善 已。

gù   yǒu wú xiāng shēng
故 有 无 相 生，

nán yì xiāng chéng
难 易 相 成，

cháng duǎn xiāng xíng
长 短 相 形，

gāo xià xiāng qīng
高 下 相 倾，

yīn shēngxiāng hè
音 声 相 和，

qián hòu xiāng suí
前 后 相 随。

shì yǐ shèng rén chǔ wú wéi zhī shì
是 以 圣 人 处 无 为 之 事，

xíng bù yán zhī jiào
行 不 言 之 教。

wàn wù zuò yān   ér   bù   cí
万 物 作 焉 而 不 辞。

shēng ér bù   yǒu
生 而 不 有，

wéi   ér   bù shì
为 而 不 恃，

gōng chéng ér   bù   jū
功 成 而 不 居。

fū   wéi fú   jū
夫 唯 弗 居，

shì yǐ bù   qù
是 以 不 去。

Laozi Passing Through the Border, by Shang Xi, Ming dynasty

老子出关图　商喜　明代(1368—1644)

It is a story about Laozi and the border officer Yin Xi. According to The Biography of Border Official Yin Xi, one day when the official mounted on the watch tower to look around, he witnessed some purple qi (some mystical energy manifested through sunshine or cloud) coming from the east. Yin Xi said, there would be a sage coming from the capital city Luoyang. When the sage was arriving, Yin Xi took an ablution and fasted. He practiced homage to see him, and requested him to write down the book now known as Daode Jing.

老子出关图，画的是李耳出关的故事。据《关令尹内传》记载：关令尹喜登楼四望，看见东方有紫气飘来。尹喜说：应该有圣人经过京邑。快到时，尹喜便斋戒沐浴。其日，果然见到老子。老子为尹喜留下五千言《道德经》。

Chapter III

Honor on man

so that none would contend for honor.

Value no rare goods

so that none would steal or rob.

Display nothing desirable

lest people be tempted and disturbed.

Therefore the sage rules

by purifying people's soul,

filling their bellies,

weakening their wills

and stengthening their bones.

He always keeps them knowledgeless

and desireless

so that the clever dare not interfere.

Where there is no interference,

there is order.

dì sān zhāng
第 三 章

bù shàng xián
不 尚 贤，

shǐ mín bù zhēng
使 民 不 争。

bù guì nán dé zhī huò
不 贵 难 得 之 货，

shǐ mín bù wéi dào
使 民 不 为 盗。

bù xiàn kě yù
不 见 可 欲，

shǐ mín xīn bù luàn
使 民 心 不 乱。

shì yǐ shèng rén zhī zhì
是 以 圣 人 之 治，

xū qí xīn
虚 其 心，

shí qí fù
实 其 腹，

ruò qí zhì
弱 其 志，

qiáng qí gǔ
强 其 骨；

cháng shǐ mín wú zhī wú yù
常 使 民 无 知 无 欲，

shǐ fú zhì zhě bù gǎn wéi yě
使 夫 智 者 不 敢 为 也。

wéi wú wéi
为 无 为，

zé wú bù zhì
则 无 不 治。

The supreme gods in Daoism are the Three Pure Ones, among whom the Heavenly Sage of Yuanshi is the highest. Yuanshi takes the meaning of "before the origin of the Universe". He is also called the Heavenly King of the Yuanshi, and resides in the Sovereign Pure Realm, which is the highest among the thirty-six levels of heaven. He is the creator of the universe, and was born before its origin. The era he dominated was the first period of the universe which is chaotic and in which yin and yang had not differentiated yet. Daoism calls this period as chaotic era. He embodies Dao and saves people from dooms.

道教最高尊神"三清"之一，又称"元始天王"、"虚皇道君"。元始天尊居三十六天之上的清微天玉清境。天尊之体长存不灭，至天地初开，受道开劫度人。他主宰和象征宇宙混沌初显、阴阳未判的第一个大世纪，道教称"混元"时期。

The Pure Jade Heavenly Lord of the Yuanshi, by an unknown author

玉清元始天尊

Chapter IV

The divine law is formless,

its use is inexhaustible.

It is endless,

whence come all things

where the sharp is blunted,

the knots are untied,

the glare is softened,

all look like dust.

Apparent,

it seems to exist.

I do not know whence it came；

it seems to exist before God.

dì sì zhāng
第 四 章

dào chōng
道 冲，

ér yòng zhī huò bù yíng
而 用 之 或 不 盈，

yuān xi
渊 兮

sì wàn wù zhī zōng
似 万 物 之 宗。

cuò qí ruì
挫 其 锐，

jiě qí fēn
解 其 纷，

hé qí guāng
和 其 光，

tóng qí chén
同 其 尘，

zhàn xi
湛 兮

sì huò cún
似 或 存。

wú bù zhī shuí zhī zǐ
吾 不 知 谁 之 子，

xiàng dì zhī xiān
象 帝 之 先。

He is one of the Three Pure Ones, who is also called "the Supreme Master of Dao". Ling Bao signifies "sacred jewel". He lives in the Supreme Realm upon the thirty-six levels of heaven. He dominates the second stage of creation, which is named Hongyuan Era.In Daoism, Lingbao gives exhortations to save people in various times.

道教最高尊神"三清"之一，又称"太上道君"。灵宝天尊居三十六天之上的禹余天上清境。道教认为"灵宝出法，随世度人"。他主宰和象征混沌始判、阴阳分明的第二个大世纪，道教称"洪元"时期。

The Heavenly Lord of the Supreme Pure Lingbao, by an unknown author

上清灵宝天尊

13

Chapter V

Heaven and earth are ruthless,

they treat everything as straw or dog.

The sage is ruthless,

he treats everyone as straw or dog.

Are not heaven and earth

like a pair of bellows?

Empty, it won't be exhausted；

Forced, more air will come out.

If more is said than done,

it would be better to take the mean.

dì wǔ zhāng
第 五 章

tiān dì bù rén
天 地 不 仁,

yǐ wàn wù wéi chú gǒu
以 万 物 为 刍 狗。

shèng rén bù rén
圣 人 不 仁,

yǐ bǎi xìng wéi chú gǒu
以 百 姓 为 刍 狗。

tiān dì zhi jiān
天 地 之 间,

qí yóu tuó yuè hū
其 犹 橐 龠 乎!

xū ér bù qū
虚 而 不 屈,

dòng ér yù chū
动 而 愈 出。

duō yán shuò qióng
多 言 数 穷,

bù rú shǒu zhōng
不 如 守 中。

Chapter VI

The vale spirit never dies.

it is the mysterious womb.

The door to the mysterious womb

is the origin of heaven and earth.

It lasts as if it ever existed；

when used, it is inexhaustible.

dì liù zhāng
第 六 章

gǔ shén bù sǐ
谷 神 不 死,

shì wèi xuán pìn
是 谓 玄 牝。

xuán pìn zhi mén
玄 牝 之 门,

shì wèi tiān dì gēn
是 谓 天 地 根。

mián mián ruò cún
绵 绵 若 存,

yòng zhi bù qín
用 之 不 勤。

He is among the Three Pure Ones, also called Supreme Master Lao, lives in the Supreme Pure Realm. He dominated the third period of creation when heaven and earth began to take their shape and everything in the universe began to evolve, and is named as Primordial Epoch. He has incarnated many times before took the form of Laozi, the founder of the Daoist School during the Spring and Autumn Period. He was given Dao from the first two sages of the Three Pure Ones, and began to spread Dao among humans. Daoists believe the works of the Three August Ones and the Five Imperial Ones, the founding of religious Daoism by Zhang Daoling, as well as the Daoist reformation by Kou Qianzhi were all conducted under his command. He is commonly recognized as the founder of Daoism.

道教最高尊神"三清"之一，又称
"太上老君"。道德天尊居三十六
天之上的大赤天太清境。他主宰
和象征天地形成、万物化生的第
三个大世纪，道教称"太初"时期。
玉清、上清、太清三位尊神皆"道
气"所化，其本皆道。太上老君历
劫化生度人，殷时聚形为老子，传
《道德》真言。后授天师张道陵正
一盟威之道，创立道教。

The Heavenly Lord of Dao and its Virtue, by an unknown author

太清道德天尊

15

Chapter VII

Heaven and earth exist for ever.

The reason why they exist so long

is not that they want to exist;

where there is no want,

to be and not to be are one.

Therefore for the sage

the last becomes the first,

the out becomes the in.

As he is selfless,

all become his self.

dì qī zhāng
第 七 章

tiān cháng dì jiǔ
天 长 地 久。

tiān dì suǒ yǐ néng
天 地 所 以 能

cháng qiě jiǔ zhě
长 且 久 者,

yǐ qí bù zì shēng
以 其 不 自 生,

gù néng cháng shēng
故 能 长 生。

shì yǐ shèng rén
是 以 圣 人

hòu qí shēn ér shēn xiān
后 其 身 而 身 先,

wài qí shēn ér shēn cún
外 其 身 而 身 存。

fēi yǐ qí wú sī xié
非 以 其 无 私 邪?

gù néng chéng qí sī
故 能 成 其 私。

The Jade Emperor is the abbreviated name for "Most Venerable Jade Emperor of the Heavenly Golden Palace" and "Lofty Jade Emperor of the Mysterious Heaven". It is believed that he was originally the Celestial God or Supreme God worshipped in early China. He is second only to the Three Pure Ones, and is the general manager of Heaven. He presides over every aspect of the celestial gods.

玉皇大帝，全称"昊天金阙无上至尊自然妙有弥罗至真玉皇大帝"，又称"玄穹高上帝"、简称"玉帝"。《云笈七签》卷三《道教本始部》称玉皇大帝是元始天尊的弟子。《玉皇本行集经》中说，玉皇为"诸天之主"、"万天之尊"，掌管三界、十方、四生六道之事。

The Jade Emperor, by an unknown author

玉皇大帝

Chapter VIII

The highest good is like water.

Water benefits everything by giving

without taking or contending.

It likes the place others dislike,

so it follows closely the divine law.

The place should be low,

the mind broad,

the gifts kind,

the speech trustworthy,

the rule sound,

the deed well-done,

the action timely.

Without contention,

a man is blameless.

dì bā zhāng
第 八 章

shàng shàn ruò shuǐ
上 善 若 水。

shuǐ shàn lì wàn wù
水 善 利 万 物

ér bù zhēng
而 不 争,

chǔ zhòng rén zhī suǒ wù
处 众 人 之 所 恶,

gù jǐ yú dào
故 几 于 道。

jū shàn dì
居 善 地,

xīn shàn yuān
心 善 渊,

yǔ shàn rén
与 善 仁,

yán shàn xìn
言 善 信,

zhèng shàn zhì
政 善 治,

shì shàn néng
事 善 能,

dòng shàn shí
动 善 时。

fú wéi bù zhēng
夫 唯 不 争,

gù wú yóu
故 无 尤。

Heavenly Master or Heavenly teacher is the honorific name for the people who attained Dao. But in latter times it refers only to Zhang Daoling and other three historical figures of Daoism, whose name are Ge Xuan, Xu Jingyang and Sa Shoujian. In Daoist temples their statues are often placed in the front of the Jade Emperor's Sanctury.

"天师"原是古代对有道者的尊称，后世道教徒尊张道陵为天师。"四大天师"为道教史上的四位重要真人，分别是张道陵、葛玄、许旌阳、萨守坚，为玉皇大帝前的四位天神。

The Four Great Heavenly Masters, by an unknown author

四大天师

Chapter IX

Don't hold your fill

but refrain from excess.

A whetted and sharpened sword

cannot be sharp for ever.

A houseful of gold and jade

cannot be safeguarded.

Arrogance of wealth and power

will bring ruin.

Withdrawal after success

conforms to the divine law.

dì jiǔ zhāng
第 九 章

chí ér yíng zhī
持 而 盈 之，

bù rú qí yǐ
不 如 其 已；

chuǎi ér ruì zhī
揣 而 锐 之，

bù kě cháng bǎo
不 可 长 保。

jīn yù mǎn táng
金 玉 满 堂，

mò zhī néng shǒu
莫 之 能 守；

fù guì ér jiāo
富 贵 而 骄，

zì yí qí jiù
自 遗 其 咎。

gōng chéng shēn tuì
功 成 身 退，

tiān zhī dào
天 之 道。

Yuanjun, which takes the meaning of "the original lady" or "the primordial sovereign", is the name for all goddesses in Daoism. Among them, the Bixia Yuanjun or the Original Lady of Emerald Cloud, the Ophthalmic Lady who has the ability to grant eyesight, the Fertile Lady who can send children to couples, the Obstetrical Lady who protects smooth bearing, and the Pox and Measles Lady who keeps pox and measles away.

道教称女神为元君。画中人物为碧霞元君及眼光娘娘、送子娘娘、催生娘娘、痘疹娘娘，传说她们能护佑人类生化长育。

Yuanjun, by an unknown author

元君像

Chapter X

Can body and soul united

never sever?

Can the controlled breath be

softened as a baby's?

Can the purified mental mirror be

free from blemish?

Can a people-loving ruler not interfere

in the state affairs?

Can the lower doors not open and close

as the upper doors in heaven?

Is it possible to understand and make

understand without knowledge?

Give life and make live,

but lay no claim,

benefit but do not interfere,

lead but do not rule,

Such is the mysterious virtue.

dì shí zhāng
第 十 章

zài yíng pò bào yī
载 营 魄 抱 一，

néng wú lí hū
能 无 离 乎？

zhuān qì zhì róu
专 气 致 柔，

néng rú yīng ér hū
能 如 婴 儿 乎？

dí chú xuán lǎn
涤 除 玄 览，

néng wú cī hū
能 无 疵 乎？

ài mín zhì guó
爱 民 治 国，

néng wú wéi hū
能 无 为 乎？

tiān mén kāi hé
天 门 开 阖，

néng wú cí hū
能 无 雌 乎？

míng bái sì dá
明 白 四 达，

néng wú zhì hū
能 无 知 乎？

shēng zhī xù zhī
生 之 蓄 之。

shēng ér bù yǒu
生 而 不 有，

wéi ér bù shì
为 而 不 恃，

zhǎng ér bù zǎi
长 而 不 宰，

shì wèi xuán dé
是 谓 玄 德。

Eighty-seven Immortals(selected), by Wu Daozi (reputedly), Tang dynasty

八十七神仙卷(局部)　吴道子(传)　唐代 (618—907)

It is regarded as the work by Wu Daozi, the great artist of Tang dynasty. Eighty-seven immortals are drawn on the picture. The figures are walking in line, having various poses and holding different things: a canopy, a flag, a lotus, a lute, a sheng (a reed pipe) or a flute. The primary and secondary are properly patterned, the civil and military are clearly differentiated. It is really a spectacular paradise scene.

《八十七神仙卷》相传是唐代著名道释人物画大师吴道子的杰作。全图 86 位神仙(边上一位被裁去)人物依序而进，人物动态各异，或执华盖，或攀幢幡，或捧莲花，或弹琵琶，或吹笙笛，主次分明，文武有别，浩浩荡荡，秩序井然，好一派庄严的天庭景象。

Chapter XI

Thirty spokes radiate from a hub.

When there is nothing in the hub,

the wheel can roll.

Turn clay to make a vessel.

When empty,

the vessel can be used.

Build a room with doors and windows.

When empty,

the room can be used as dwelling.

When there is something, it is beneficial;

When empty, it is useful.

dì shí yī zhāng
第 十 一 章

sān shí fú gòng yī gǔ
三 十 辐 共 一 毂,

dāng qí wú
当 其 无,

yǒu chē zhī yòng
有 车 之 用;

yán zhí yǐ wéi qì
埏 植 以 为 器,

dāng qí wú
当 其 无,

yǒu qì zhī yòng
有 器 之 用;

záo hù yǒu yǐ wéi shì
凿 户 牖 以 为 室,

dāng qí wú
当 其 无,

yǒu shì zhī yòng
有 室 之 用。

gù yǒu zhī yǐ wéi lì
故 有 之 以 为 利,

wú zhī yǐ wéi yòng
无 之 以 为 用。

By a brook, and among some bamboos, there are two red-crowned cranes, whose postures are beautiful, and expressions are leisurely and free. This is the lifestyle for which people long. Cranes, according to Daoism are often the vehicles for immortals on which people can ascend to the heaven; and they are often the partners of immortals in Daoist paintings. Hence cranes are the symbols of transcendence and primitive simplicity. Cranes are the auspicious birds in Chinese culture.

画中溪水之畔、翠竹之间，两只丹顶白鹤，形态优美，悠然自在。这正是人们向往的生活状态。在道画中神仙旁常有鹤相伴，鹤也因此成为超脱飘逸，返璞自然的象征。鹤在道教中常为仙人坐骑，载人飞入天界。故人们将鹤看成是吉祥之鸟。

Twin Cranes, by Bian Jingzhao, Ming dynasty

双鹤图　边景昭　明代

25

Chapter XII

The five colors may confuse the eye.

The five sounds may deafen the ear.

The five tastes may spoil the palate.

Riding and hunting may madden the

mind.

Rare goods may tempt one to do evil.

Therefore the sage satisfies the belly

rather than the eye.

He prefers the former to the latter.

dì shí èr zhāng
第 十 二 章

wǔ sè lìng rén mù máng
五 色 令 人 目 盲,

wǔ yin lìng rén ěr lóng
五 音 令 人 耳 聋,

wǔ wèi lìng rén kǒu shuǎng
五 味 令 人 口 爽,

chí chěng tián liè
驰 骋 畋 猎,

lìng rén xin fā kuáng
令 人 心 发 狂,

nán dé zhī huò
难 得 之 货,

lìng rén xing fáng
令 人 行 妨。

shì yǐ shèng rén wèi fù bù wèi mù
是 以 圣 人 为 腹 不 为 目,

gù qù bǐ qǔ cǐ
故 去 彼 取 此。

Shuilu means literally water and land. They are ritual paintings originally introduced by Buddhism from India in the periods of Wei State and Jin dynasty. Thereafter, people have got used to calling the paintings of deities hung on the Daoist liturgical altar as altar painting. Now all Buddhist and Daoist liturgical paintings of deities which are made according to uniform patterns are designated as Shuilu paintings.

水陆画，最早出现在魏晋时期，最初用于佛教水陆道场。后来人们习惯将道教用于法事活动时悬挂于神坛的神像画，也称为水陆画。现在则将由画工所作的、有统一模式，用于宗教活动，反映神、佛内容的绘画统称为水陆画。

Shuilu Painting-the Gods of the Five Directions and the God of Mount Changbai, Ming dynasty

五方五帝长白山间天仙圣帝（水陆画）　明代

Chapter XIII

Praise and blame disturb the mind;

Fortune and misfortune affect the body.

Why is the mind disturbed?

Praise and blame are like

ups and downs.

The mind is troubled

with rise and fall.

So is it troubled by praise and blame.

How can fortune and misfortune

affect the body?

Because we have a body.

If we had not a body.

how can we be affected?

If you value the world as your body,

then the world may confide in you.

If you love the world as your body,

then the world may be entrusted to you.

dì shí sān zhāng
第 十 三 章

chǒng rǔ ruò jīng
宠 辱 若 惊，

guì dà huàn ruò shēn
贵 大 患 若 身。

hé wèi chǒng rǔ ruò jīng
何 谓 宠 辱 若 惊？

chǒng wéi shàng
宠 为 上，

rǔ wéi xià
辱 为 下。

dé zhī ruò jīng
得 之 若 惊，

shī zhī ruò jīng
失 之 若 惊，

shì wèi chǒng rǔ ruò jīng
是 谓 宠 辱 若 惊。

hé wèi guì dà huàn ruò shēn
何 谓 贵 大 患 若 身？

wú suǒ yǐ yǒu dà huàn zhě
吾 所 以 有 大 患 者，

wèi wú yǒu shēn
为 吾 有 身，

jí wú wú shēn
及 吾 无 身，

wú yǒu hé huàn
吾 有 何 患。

gù guì yǐ shēn wèi tiān xià
故 贵 以 身 为 天 下，

zé kě jì tiān xià
则 可 寄 天 下。

ài yǐ shēn wèi tiān xià
爱 以 身 为 天 下，

zé kě tuō tiān xià
则 可 托 天 下。

The Gods of Cities are called Chenghuang, which means the god of walls and moats. The city gods are often historical local officials who have rendered outstanding services. The responsibilities of the Gods of Villages are in charge of the local small pieces of land, judging the residents' merits, protecting the local community from attack and relieving drought and flood. The access to the deities by the Daoist liturgical messages is also transmitted through the god of local place.

道教奉主管城池的神为城隍。各地城隍多为保卫该地区有功之人。掌管大地之神为土地神。

The Gods of Cities and Villages, by an unknown author, Ming dynasty

诸郡城隍诸司土地之神　明代

Chapter XIV

What cannot be seen is invisible,

What cannot be heard is inaudible,

What cannot be touched is intangible.

These there, unfathomable,

blend into one.

Up, it is not bright；

down, it is not dark.

Like a nameless endless string,

it ends in nothing.

It is a formless form,

an image of nothing.

It seems to be and not to be.

Before it, you cannot see its front；

after it, you cannot see its rear.

Ruling over the present with the law of

the past,

you can know the beginning of antiquity.

Such is the rule of the divine law.

dì shí sì zhāng
第 十 四 章

shì zhī bù jiàn míng yuē yí
视 之 不 见 名 曰 夷,

tīng zhī bù wén míng yuē xī
听 之 不 闻 名 曰 希,

bó zhī bù dé míng yuē wēi
搏 之 不 得 名 曰 微。

cǐ sān zhě bù kě zhì jié
此 三 者 不 可 致 诘,

gù hùn ér wéi yī
故 混 而 为 一。

qí shàng bù jiǎo
其 上 不 徼,

qí xià bù mèi
其 下 不 昧,

shéng shéng bù kě míng
绳 绳 不 可 名,

fù guī yú wù wú
复 归 于 无 物。

shì wèi wú zhuàng zhī zhuàng
是 谓 无 状 之 状,

wú wù zhī xiàng
无 物 之 象,

shì wèi hū huǎng
是 谓 惚 恍。

yíng zhī bù jiàn qí shǒu
迎 之 不 见 其 首,

suí zhī bù jiàn qí hòu
随 之 不 见 其 后。

zhí gǔ zhī dào
执 古 之 道,

yǐ yù jīn zhī yǒu
以 御 今 之 有。

néng zhī gǔ shǐ
能 知 古 始,

shì wèi dào jì
是 谓 道 纪。

They are the deities or spirits of myriad things, e.g. the Sun, the Moon, constellations, animals and plants.

道教认为世间万事万物均有神灵主宰，故日、月、星、辰、山川岳渎、动物、植物等等均有主管神灵。

The Divine General of the Steppe and the Gods of Waters and Lands, by an unknown author, Ming dynasty

旷野大将水陆圣导等神众　明代

Chapter XV

The ancients followed the divine law,

subtle, delicate, mysterious,

communicative,

too deep to be understood.

Not objectively understood,

it can only be subjectively described.

The ancients were circumspect as crossing

a frozen river,

watchful as fearful of hostile neighbors,

reserved as an unacquainted guest,

softened as melting ice,

natural as uncarved block,

vacant as a vale,

and obscure as a muddy stream.

Who could calm the turbid water?

It could be slowly turned clean.

Who could stir the stale water?

It could be slowly revived.

Those who follow the divine law

will not be full to the brim.

Only those who do not go to excess

can renew what is worn out.

dì shí wǔ zhāng
第 十 五 章

gǔ zhī shàn wéi dào zhě
古 之 善 为 道 者，

wēi miào xuán tōng
微 妙 玄 通，

shēn bù kě shí
深 不 可 识。

fú wéi bù kě shí
夫 唯 不 可 识，

gù qiǎng wèi zhī róng
故 强 为 之 容。

yùxì ruò dōng shè chuān
豫 兮 若 冬 涉 川；

yóu xi ruò wèi sì lín
犹 兮 若 畏 四 邻；

yǎn xi qí ruò róng
俨 兮 其 若 容；

huàn xi ruò bīng zhī jiāng shì
涣 兮 若 冰 之 将 释；

dūn xi qí ruò pǔ
敦 兮 其 若 朴；

kuàng xi qí ruò gǔ
旷 兮 其 若 谷；

hún xi qí ruò zhuó
混 兮 其 若 浊；

shú néng zhuó yǐ jìng zhī
孰 能 浊 以 静 之？

xú qīng
徐 清。

shú néng ān yǐ dòng zhī
孰 能 安 以 动 之？

xú shēng
徐 生。

bǎo cǐ dào zhě bù yù yíng
保 此 道 者 不 欲 盈。

fú wéi bù yíng
夫 唯 不 盈，

gù néng bì ěr xīn chéng
故 能 蔽 而 新 成。

The Four Immortals Saluting to the Longevity Constellation, by Shang Xi, Ming dynasty

四仙拱寿图　商喜　明代

This picture depicts that the four legendary figures in Daoism and Buddhism are saluting the Longevity Constellation who is riding on a crane, while crossing the sea. The four immortals are Iron Crutch Li who is among the most popular Eight Immortals and holding a gourd, Liu Haichan who is riding on a toad, Han Shan and Shi De who are two Zen Buddhist Masters capable of poetry and often pretend to be crackbrained. The strokes has some flavor of "strips in Wu Daozi's work being blown in wind" (Wu Daozi is a famous painter in Tang dynasty), and has the hints of influence of paintings in Song and Yuan dynasties. Gauffers of the characters' robes are waving and twisted with wind, which seem to have rendered the skill of "Cracked Reeds" in that the strokes are unrestrained, rhythmic and vigorous. The sea waves are drawn with the skill of "vibrant strokes" (Zhanbi) and have a good decoration effect.

此图描绘佛、道教传说人物渡海，巧遇骑鹤之寿星老人。图中有八仙之一里李铁拐，全真教五祖之一刘海蟾，及颠狂、好吟词偈之唐朝禅僧寒山与拾得。本幅画传承唐朝吴道子"吴带当风"之画法，并受宋、元简笔禅画之影响。人物衣纹飘举转折近似"折芦法"，用笔锋芒毫纵、顿挫有力。海涛以战笔勾描，颇具装饰性。

Chapter XVI

Do your utmost to be empty-minded

and hold fast to tranquillity.

All things grow,

I see them return to nature.

Multiple as things are,

they return to their root.

Their root is tranquillity；

to return to it is their destiny.

To submit to one's destiny is the rule；

to know the rule is wisdom.

Those who act against the rule

will harm themselves.

Those who understand will pardon,

and to pardon is justice.

Justice is perfect,

and perfection belongs to heaven.

Heaven is the divine law,

and the divine law is eternal.

Men may pass away, but the law will

never.

dì shí liù zhāng
第 十 六 章

zhì xū jí
致 虚 极，

shǒu jìng dǔ
守 静 笃。

wàn wù bìng zuò
万 物 并 作，

wú yǐ guān fù
吾 以 观 复。

fú wù yún yún
夫 物 芸 芸，

gè fù guī qí gēn
各 复 归 其 根。

guī gēn yuē jìng
归 根 曰 静，

shì wèi fù mìng
是 谓 复 命。

fù mìng yuē cháng
复 命 曰 常，

zhī cháng yuē míng
知 常 曰 明。

bù zhī cháng
不 知 常，

wàng zuò xiōng
妄 作 凶。

zhī cháng róng
知 常 容，

róng nǎi gōng
容 乃 公，

gōng nǎi quán
公 乃 全，

quán nǎi tiān
全 乃 天，

tiān nǎi dào
天 乃 道，

dào nǎi jiǔ
道 乃 久。

mò shēn bú dài
殁 身 不 殆。

The Portrait of the Perfected Man Taiyi, selected from the frescos in Yongle Palace, Yuan dynasty

太乙真人像　永乐宫壁画(局部)　元代 (1206—1368)

Taiyies are among the constellation gods worshipped by Daoists. The Pilgrimage to the Original Lords is a fresco in Yongle Palace, on which there are ten Taiyies, who are standing beside the Queen Mother of the West.

道教尊祀的星神。《朝元图》中绘有十位太乙，分立于金母元君两侧。

Chapter XVII

What is the best rule?

None knows there is a ruler.

What is the second best?

The ruler is loved and praised.

What comes next?

He is feared.

Still next?

He is disobeyed.

For he is not trustworthy enough

or not at all.

For long he should spare his speech.

When things are done,

he should let people say that all is

natural.

dì shí qī zhāng
第 十 七 章

tài shàng
太 上，

bù zhī yǒu zhī
不 知 有 之。

qí cì
其 次，

qīn ér yù zhī
亲 而 誉 之。

qí cì
其 次，

wèi zhī
畏 之。

qí cì
其 次，

wǔ zhī
侮 之。

xìn bù zú yān
信 不 足 焉，

yǒu bù xìn yān
有 不 信 焉。

yōu xī qí guì yán
悠 兮 其 贵 言，

gōng chéng shì suì
功 成 事 遂，

bǎi xìng jiē wèi wǒ zì rán
百 姓 皆 谓 我 自 然。

They are two unauspicious constellations in Daoist astrology, who are the incarnations of the Uranus and Big Dipper, and hence the two ambassadors of the two constellations. They are named in this way because one of them is portrayed as holding a goat, while the other holding a Mandragora flower, which is poisonous and hallucinogenic.

擎羊、陀罗乃天皇星、紫微星所气化，
为天皇、紫微的两大使者。

The Ambassadors of Goat and Mandragora, by unknown author

擎羊陀罗使者

Chapter XVIII

When the divine law is not followed,

good and just men are needed.

When falsehood is practised,

true and wise men are needed.

When the family is at odds,

filial sons and kind parents are

needed.

When the state is at stake,

loyal officials are needed.

dì shí bā zhāng
第 十 八 章

dà dào fèi
大 道 废，

yǒu rén yì
有 仁 义；

huì zhì chū
慧 智 出，

yǒu dà wěi
有 大 伪；

liù qīn bù hé
六 亲 不 和，

yǒu xiào cí
有 孝 慈；

guó jiā hūn luàn
国 家 昏 乱，

yǒu zhōng chén
有 忠 臣。

The Iron-Foot Daoist Master, by Shi Tao, Qing dynasty

铁脚道人图　石涛　清代（1616—1911）

The Iron Foot Daoist Master is a legendary immortal. He walk with his bare feet, ate plum flowers with snow to let the cold fragrance to rinse the inner organs. The picture is about a story that once he climbed upon the summit of South Sacred Mountain, Zhurong Peak, whistled and has gone with wind. The inscription says that the author has mounted Mount Huang, and begun to believe that it is the real peak in the world. He also whistled but could not fly away with wind. This picture presents his devout will to practice Dao.

铁脚道人传说是一位神仙，图中描绘其赤脚行路，嚼梅花，沁心脾，登南岳衡山顶峰—祝融峰仰天长啸后，飘然而去的故事。题识上说，作者自己曾登黄山始信峰，也曾长啸，但此身无论如何也没能飘然，表达了作者渴望修道成仙的心愿。

Chapter XIX

If sagacity were not praised,

people would be benefited a hundredfold.

If morality were not advocated.

sons would be filial and parents kind.

If ill-gotten wealth were rejected,

no thieves or robbers would appear.

These there things

should not be adorned in good words.

So the following rules should be observed:

be simple and plain,

selfless and desireless,

unlearned and unworried.

dì shí jiǔ zhāng
第 十 九 章

jué shèng qì zhì
绝 圣 弃 智，

mín lì bǎi bèi
民 利 百 倍；

jué rén qì yì
绝 仁 弃 义，

mín fù xiào cí
民 复 孝 慈；

jué qiǎo qì lì
绝 巧 弃 利，

dào zéi wú yǒu
盗 贼 无 有；

cǐ sān zhě
此 三 者，

yǐ wéi wén bù zú
以 为 文 不 足，

gù lìng yǒu suǒ shǔ
故 令 有 所 属：

jiàn sù bào pǔ
见 素 抱 朴，

shǎo sī guǎ yù
少 私 寡 欲，

jué xué wú yōu
绝 学 无 忧。

The Holyland of Mount Huang, by Shi Tao, Qing dynasty

黄山胜境　石涛　清代

The three immortals are perching on the crown of the old pine which is growing on the rocky peak. They are talking or watching leisurely as if they are going to fly away with wind. It is a carefree and ethereal world.

三位仙人憩于山峰奇松顶上，超脱飘然，轻松自在，或促膝交谈，或极目远眺，画中三位仙人似随时有飘然飞去之感。

Chapter XX

How far away

is yes from no?

How far away

is good from evil?

What others fear,

can I not fear?

How far are they from the center?

The multitude are merry

as enjoying a sacrificial feast.

or climbing the height in spring.

Alone I am so inactive as to show no sign,

innocent

as a baby who cannot smile,

indifferent

as a homeless wanderer.

All men have more than enough；

alone I seem to have noting left over.

What I have is a fool's heart!

dì èr shí zhāng
第 二 十 章

wéi zhī yǔ ē
唯 之 与 阿,

xiāng qù jǐ hé
相 去 几 何?

shàn zhī yǔ è
善 之 与 恶,

xiāng qù ruò hé
相 去 若 何?

rén zhī suǒ wèi
人 之 所 畏,

bù kě bù wèi
不 可 不 畏。

huāng xi qí wèi yāng zāi
荒 兮 其 未 央 哉!

zhòng rén xi xi
众 人 熙 熙,

rú xiǎng tài láo
如 享 太 牢,

rú chūn dēng tái
如 春 登 台。

wǒ dú bó xi qí wèi zhào
我 独 泊 兮 其 未 兆,

dùn dùn xi
沌 沌 兮

rú yīng ér zhī wèi hái
如 婴 儿 之 未 孩,

They are duty gods respectively in charge of the year, the month, the day and the hour. They keep records of the heaven, earth and humans, and report to the Jade Emperor. Besides, all sacrificial memorials burnt in the liturgies have to be submitted to them before the heavenly lords' accesses.

道教所奉值年、值月、值日、值时的四位天神叫四值功曹。他们职掌三界十方的功过，向玉皇大帝禀奏。另外凡是人间"上达天庭"的表文，焚烧之后也要经过他们之手呈递上天。

The Four Duty Gods, by unknown author, Qing dynasty

四值功曹　清代

The vulgar seem in the light；

alone I am in the dark.

The vulgar seem observant；

alone I am dull.

The multitude are useful；

alone I am useless and indolent.

Different from others,

I value the mother* who feeds.

* the divine law

léi léi xī ruò wú suǒ guī
累 累 兮 若 无 所 归!

zhòng rén jiē yǒu yú
众 人 皆 有 余,

ér wǒ dú ruò yí
而 我 独 若 遗。

wǒ yú rén zhī xīn yě zāi
我 愚 人 之 心 也 哉,

sú rén zhāo zhāo
俗 人 昭 昭,

wǒ dú hūn hūn
我 独 昏 昏;

sú rén chá chá
俗 人 察 察,

wǒ dú mèn mèn
我 独 闷 闷。

dàn xī qí ruò hǎi
澹 兮 其 若 海,

liáo xī ruò wú zhǐ
蓼 兮 若 无 止。

zhòng rén jiē yǒu yǐ
众 人 皆 有 以,

ér wǒ dú wán sì bǐ
而 我 独 顽 似 鄙。

wǒ dú yì yú rén
我 独 异 于 人,

ér guì shí mǔ
而 贵 食 母。

A Flying Immortal (selected), by Zhao Boju, Song dynasty

飞仙图(局部) 赵伯驹 宋代

The immortals in Daoism are not limited by time and space. They have free and wondering lives, and their wisdom is unfathomable. They "climbs up on the clouds and mist, rides a flying dragon, and wanders beyond the four seas", which are the imaginations of immortal. This is just a presentation of the visions: the immortal is riding on a dragon, with a lotus in hand, and is hovering over the fairy islands and seas.

道教的神仙，生存不受时空的限制，生活逍遥自在，智能神妙莫测。"乘云气御飞龙，而游呼四海之外"，就是一般观念中的神仙体相。此画云中仙人持荷花乘龙，翱翔于海山瑶岛，正是古代想象中的仙人。

Chapter XXI

The content of great virtue

conforms to the divine law.

The divine law is something

which seems to be and not to be.

What seems to exist and does not exist?

It is the image.

What seems not to exist but exists?

It is the image of something.

What seems deep and dark?

It is the essence.

The essence is very true,

for we believe in it.

From ancient times to present day

its name cannot be erased

so that we know the fathers of all things.

How can I know

what these fathers look like?

By means of this.

kǒng dé zhī róng
孔 德 之 容,

wéi dào shì cóng
惟 道 是 从。

dào zhī wéi wù
道 之 为 物,

wéi huǎng wéi hū
惟 恍 惟 惚。

hū xī huǎng xī
惚 兮 恍 兮,

qí zhōng yǒu xiàng
其 中 有 象。

huǎng xī hū xī
恍 兮 惚 兮,

qí zhōng yǒu wù
其 中 有 物。

yǎo xī míng xī
窈 兮 冥 兮,

qí zhōng yǒu jīng
其 中 有 精。

qí jīng shèn zhēn
其 精 甚 真,

qí zhōng yǒu xìn
其 中 有 信。

zì gǔ jí jīn
自 古 及 今,

qí míng bù qù
其 名 不 去,

yǐ yuè zhòng fǔ
以 阅 众 甫。

wú hé yǐ zhī zhòng fǔ zhī zhuàng zāi
吾 何 以 知 众 甫 之 状 哉?

yǐ cǐ
以 此。

It is a collection of the constellation gods: the Constellations of Happiness, Success and Longevity; The nine luminaries: the five planets (Mars, Mercury, Jupiter, Venus and Saturn), also Rahu, the spirit that causes eclipses, and Ketu, a comet, the purple Qi and the Yuedu (the last two are the substitutes for the Sun and the Moon of the similar theory in Buddhism); the twenty-eight ecliptic mansions; and the twelve palaces.

万寿福禄：即福神、禄神、寿神三位神仙。

九曜：即金、木、水、火、土、罗侯、计度、紫气、月度九位神仙。

二十八宿：中国古代的星象学家把太阳和月亮经过的天区叫做"黄道"，并把黄道中星宿分为二十八个星座，每个星座都有一个天将即二十八宿。

十二宫：为降娄、大梁、实沈、鹑首、鹑头、鹑尾、寿星、大火、析木、星纪、玄号、娵訾。十二宫即黄道周天的十二段。

The Gods of Constellations, by an unknown author, Ming dynasty

万寿福禄九曜二十八宿十二宫神众　明代

Chapter XXII

Stooping, you will be preserved.

Wronged, you will be righted.

Hollow, you will be filled.

Worn out, you will be renewed.

Having little, you may gain；

having much, you may be at a loss.

So the sage holds on to one

to be the model for the world.

He does not show himself,

so he is seen everywhere.

He does not assert himself,

dì èr shí èr zhāng
第 二 十 二 章

qū zé quán
曲 则 全，

wǎng zé zhí
枉 则 直，

wā zé yíng
洼 则 盈，

bì zé xin
敝 则 新，

shǎo zé dé
少 则 得，

duō zé huò
多 则 惑。

shì yǐ shèng rén bào yī wéi tiān xià shì
是 以 圣 人 抱 一 为 天 下 式。

bù zì xiàn
不 自 见，

gù míng
故 明；

The Earthly Queen of the Land Gods, selected from Yongle Palace, Yuan dynasty

承天效法后土皇地祇　永乐宫壁画(局部)　元代

It is also called Queen Earth in abbreviation. She is responsible for the interchange of yin and yang, population growth, and beauty (especially of natural scenery). She is often grouped with the Jade Emperor, and as a pair they are called the "Emperor Heaven and the Queen Earth". The image of Queen Earth is similar to that of ancient Chinese queens. She is affable and elegant, with a phoenix coronet on her head and an embroidered cape draped over her shoulders.

承天效法后土皇地祇是道教尊神"四御"中的第四位天神，简称"后土"，俗称"后土娘娘"。与主持天界的玉皇大帝相配合，为主宰大地山川生育的女神。后土信仰源于中国古代对土地的崇拜。

49

so he is well-known.

He does not boast,

so he wins success.

He is not proud,

so he can lead.

As he contends for nothing,

none in the world could contend with him.

Is it not true for the ancients to say,

"Stooping, you will be preserved" ?

It is indeed the whole truth to which lead

all the ways.

bù zì shì
不自是，

gù zhāng
故彰；

bù zì fá
不自伐，

gù yǒu gōng
故有功；

bù zì jīn
不自矜，

gù cháng
故长；

fú wéi bù zhēng
夫惟不争，

gù tiān xià mò néng yǔ zhī zhēng
故天下莫能与之争。

gǔ zhī suǒ wèi qū zé quán zhě
古之所谓曲则全者，

qǐ xū yán zāi
岂虚言哉！

chéng quán ér guī zhī
诚全而归之。

An Illustration to the Ode for Goddess of Luo River "selected", by Gu Kaizi, East Jin dynasty

洛神赋(局部)　顾恺之　东晋 (317-420)

The Ode for the Goddess of Luo River is a famous poem by Caozhi in the Three-Kingdom period (220~265), who was the son of the Prime Minister Cao Cao. It depicts the love story between the Goddess of Luo River and the author, which happens on his way home from the capital. Clustered round by his attendants, Cao Zhi stops and dismounts by the river side to have a rest. The breeze and ripples make him feel gloomy and chant a poem, moving the river goddess. Dressed in long and soft skirt and with high hair temples, she comes out from the water, floats close to him serenely and gently. Her eyes stare into his eyes passionately. She sings and dances in the sky and upon the mountains for him. After that, she leaves on a vehicle slowly but looks back again and again. The poet and his attendants see her off until she disappears. This is a commonly aspired story of illustration paintings among the literati in old times.

《洛神赋》是中国三国时期文学家曹植的名篇，描述作者在由京师返回途中与洛水女神相遇的恋爱故事。画中，曹植在侍卫仆从的簇拥下，来到洛水边下马暂息，面对洛水微波，惆怅徘徊、神情忧郁，水面上女神头梳高髻，仪静柔情飘浮而来，目光顾盼，欲行又止。洛水女神在天空在山间舒袖歌舞，曹植携随从相送，凝目远视，女神最终乘车慢慢离去。此画即是描绘的这则故事，也是后代文人、画家们常用来抒发心情和书画的题材。

51

Chapter XXIII

It is natural to speak little.

A wanton wind cannot whisper all the

morning；

a sudden rain cannot howl all the day long.

Who has made them so?

Heaven and earth.

Heaven and earth cannot speak long,

not to speak of man.

Therefore, those who follow the divine law

conform to it；

so do those who follow the human law,

and those who imitate heaven.

Those who conform to the divine law

are welcome to the divine；

those who conform to the human law

are welcome to the human；

those who confron to heaven.

are welcome to the heaven.

Some are not trustworthy enough,

some, not at all.

dì èr shí sān zhāng
第 二 十 三 章

xī yán zì rán
希 言 自 然，

gù piāo fēng bù zhōng zhāo
故 飘 风 不 终 朝，

zhòu yǔ bù zhōng rì
骤 雨 不 终 日。

shú wéi cǐ zhě
孰 为 此 者？

tiān dì
天 地。

tiān dì shàng bù néng jiǔ
天 地 尚 不 能 久，

ér kuàng yú rén hū
而 况 于 人 乎？

gù cóng shì yú dào zhě
故 从 事 于 道 者，

tóng yú dào
同 于 道；

yú dé zhě tóng yú dé
于 德 者，同 于 德。

yú zhě zhě tóng yú tiān
于 天 者，同 于 天。

tóng yú dào zhě
同 于 道 者，

dào yì lè dé zhī
道 亦 乐 得 之；

tóng yú dé zhě
同 于 德 者，

dé yì lè dé zhī
德 亦 乐 得 之；

tóng yú tiān zhě
同 于 天 者，

tiān yì lè dé zhī
天 亦 乐 得 之。

xìn bù zú yān
信 不 足 焉，

yǒu bù xìn yān
有 不 信 焉。

They Marshal of Wind names Zhou Guang, and the Marshal of Chaos Pang Qiao. They are two among the thirty-six divine generals.

风轮元帅 混气元帅为道教三十六天将神之一，风轮元帅名周广，混气元帅名庞乔。

The Marshal of the Wind and the Marshal of Chaos, by an unknown author, Qing dynasty

风轮元帅　混气元帅　清代

Chapter XXIV

One who stands on tiptoe cannot stand firm；

who makes big strides cannot walk long.

One who sees only himself has no good

sight；

who thinks only himself right cannot be

recognized.

One who boasts of himself will not succeed；

who thinks himself superior cannot be a

leader.

In the light of the divine law

such behavior is like superfluous food.

It is disliked

by those who follow the divine law.

dì èr shí sì zhāng
第 二 十 四 章

qǐ zhě bù lì
企 者 不 立，

kuà zhě bù xíng
跨 者 不 行。

zì jiàn zhě bù míng
自 见 者 不 明，

zì shì zhě bù zhāng
自 是 者 不 彰，

zì fá zhě wú gōng
自 伐 者 无 功，

zì jīn zhě bù cháng
自 矜 者 不 长。

qí zài dào yě
其 在 道 也，

yuē yú shí zhuì xíng
曰：余 食 赘 行。

wù huò wù zhi
物 或 恶 之，

gù yǒu dào zhě bù chǔ
故 有 道 者 不 处。

The Convocation of Deities by Heavenly Master Zhang (Selected), by an unknown author, Ming dynasty

张天师请神图（局部）　明代

Zhang Daoling, the founder of the religious Daoism, is also named as the Heavenly Master of Exorcism and Apologetics. In this picture, he is performing the liturgies to summon the deities, and the Daoist priests and lay people are observing quietly and concentratedly in queues.

张天师即道教的创始人张道陵，又称降魔护道天师。图绘其正在做法请神、众道士、护法排列整齐，静心定观。

Chapter XXV

There was chaos

before the existence of heaven and earth.

Void and vast,

independent and changeless,

moving in cycle,

it may be the mother of heaven and earth.

I do not know its name

and call it the divine law

or perfunctorily style it the great.

The great will pass away,

passing implies a long way,

and however long, the way will return in the end.

So the divine law is great,

so are heaven and earth,

and so is man.

There are four things great in the universe,

and man is one of them.

Man imitates earth,

earth imitates heaven,

heaven follows the divine law,

and the divine law follows nature.

dì èr shí wǔ zhāng
第 二 十 五 章

yǒu wù hún chéng
有 物 混 成,

xiān tiān dì shēng
先 天 地 生。

jì xī liáo xī
寂 兮 寥 兮,

dú lì bù gǎi
独 立 不 改,

zhōu xíng ér bù dài
周 行 而 不 殆,

kě yǐ wéi tiān dì mǔ
可 以 为 天 地 母。

wú bù zhī qí míng
吾 不 知 其 名,

zì zhī yuē dào
字 之 曰 道。

qiǎng wèi zhī míng yuē dà
强 为 之 名 曰 大。

dà yuē shì
大 曰 逝,

shì yuē yuǎn
逝 曰 远,

yuǎn yuē fǎn
远 曰 反。

gù dào dà
故 道 大,

tiān dà dì dà
天 大 地 大,

rén yì dà
人 亦 大。

yù zhōng yǒu sì dà
域 中 有 四 大,

ér rén jū qí yī yān
而 人 居 其 一 焉。

rén fǎ dì
人 法 地,

dì fǎ tiān
地 法 天,

tiān fǎ dào
天 法 道,

dào fǎ zì rán
道 法 自 然。

Constellations of Happiness, Success and Longevity, by an unknown author, Ming Dynasty

福禄寿星众（局部） 明代

They are the three constellations in folklores, but in Daoism they are called as Tianguan (the Heavenly Official), the God of Literati and the God of Longevity. The Heavenly Official is the God of Blessing who can confer blessings, the God of Literati can confer promotions and the God of Longevity is the Constellation of South Pole and symbol for a long live. As Chinese genre paintings, they are often pasted by common families to pray for blessings.

民间传说中的"福"、"禄"、"寿"三位星君，即道教信奉的天官、文昌和寿星。据说"天官赐福"，故为福神；文昌主加官进禄；寿星即南极仙人翁，乃长寿之象征，为寿神。中国民间多绘有他们三位的画像，以求福求禄求寿。

Chapter XXVI

The heavy is the base of the light；
the still is the lord of the rash.
So the sage goes all day long
without leaving his heavy baggage.
Though with glory in view,
he stays light-hearted.
Why should a ruler of ten thousand
chariots make light of the country?
Light, the base will be lost；
so will be a rash ruler.

dì   èr   shí   liù   zhāng
第 二 十 六 章

zhòng wéi qīng gēn
重 为 轻 根，

jìng wéi zào jūn
静 为 躁 君。

shì   yǐ shèng rén zhōng rì xíng
是 以 圣 人 终 日 行

bù   lí   zī zhòng
不 离 辎 重。

suī yǒu róng guān
虽 有 荣 观，

yàn chù chāo rán
燕 处 超 然。

nài   hé wàn shèng zhī zhǔ
奈 何 万 乘 之 主，

ér   yǐ shēn qīng tiān xià
而 以 身 轻 天 下？

qīng zé   shī gēn
轻 则 失 根，

zào zé   shī jūn
躁 则 失 君。

Iron Crutch Li or Li Tieguai, is the most ancient of the Eight Immortals, because he lived in Western Zhou dynasty. Prior to being an immortal, his spirit once traveled to the heaven; his disciple was told that the spirit will return in seven days, but on the sixth day, the disciple's mother was in grave illness, he had to return home, so he cremated the body. Upon returning, Li had no choice but to enter the corpse of a beggar who died of starvation. Unfortunately the man's head was long and pointed, his face black, his beard and hair woolly and disheveled, his eyes of gigantic size, and one of his legs was lame. Laozi gave him a gold band to keep his hair in order, and an iron crutch to help his lame leg. So the crutch becomes his recognized emblem. The other miraculous thing is the bottle-gourd or calabash with medicines inside and hence with fabled properties for healing. The gourd also has other mysterious functions such as absorbing people' s soul (hun) and mirroring the past and future. After he had renovated his merit records, he was ranked as superior immortals by the Jade Emperor.

李铁拐，八仙之一，又称铁拐李。其形象魁伟，遁隐于山洞中，常背一葫芦，浪迹江湖，行医治病，后功行圆满，被玉皇大帝封为上仙。

Iron Crutch Li, by an unknown author, Yuan dynasty

李铁拐像　元代

Chapter XXVII

Good deeds leave no traces.

Good words exclude mistakes.

Good at counting, none uses counters.

A good lock without a bolt

cannot be opened.

A good knot tied without strings

cannot be untied.

Therefore, a sage is good

at helping people

without rejecting anyone.

He is good at saving things

without abandoning anything.

dì èr shí qī zhāng
第 二 十 七 章

shàn xíng wú zhé jì
善 行 无 辙 迹，

shàn yán wú xiá zhé
善 言 无 瑕 谪，

shàn shù bù yòng chóu cè
善 数 不 用 筹 策，

shàn bì wú guān jiàn
善 闭 无 关 楗，

ér bù kě kāi
而 不 可 开，

shàn jié wú shéng yuē
善 结 无 绳 约，

ér bù kě jiě
而 不 可 解。

shì yǐ shèng rén cháng shàn jiù rén
是 以 圣 人 常 善 救 人，

gù wú qì rén
故 无 弃 人；

cháng shàn jiù wù
常 善 救 物，

gù wú qì wù
故 无 弃 物。

A Musician Lady, selected from frescos in Yongle Palace, Yuan dynasty

乐女　永乐宫壁画(局部)　元代

It is one of the musician ladies painted on the arch panels of the niche for the statue of Lu Dongbin, in Chunyang Sanctury, Yongle Palace. The strokes are quite simple, the hues are harmonious, which are important documents for ancient music studies.

永乐宫纯阳殿中间有一座供奉吕洞宾塑像的神龛，龛顶的东、西、北三面拱眼上，绘有手持不同乐器的乐女，笔法简炼、色调和谐，是研究古乐的重要资料。

This is called invisible wisdom.

Thus a sage is

the teacher of common people,

and the common people

are the stuff for good men.

If the teacher is not honored

and the stuff not valued,

even a wise man will be at a loss.

This is the essential secret.

shì wèi xí míng
是 谓 袭 明。

gù shàn rén zhě
故 善 人 者,

bù shàn rén zhī shī
不 善 人 之 师;

bù shàn rén zhě
不 善 人 者,

shàn rén zhī zī
善 人 之 资。

bù guì qí shī
不 贵 其 师,

bù ài qí zī
不 爱 其 资。

suī zhì dà mí
虽 智 大 迷,

shì wèi yào miào
是 谓 要 妙。

Yama is the lord of death whose first recorded appearance is in the Vedas. But the Yamas in ten halls is unique in China. The Yamas in different halls have various responsibilities: one determines people's life span, one records merits, one grant lucks or mishaps, one guides delivery and one punishes the criminals. It is a very popular belief among Chinese common people. It tells that the spirits of the dead, on being judged by Yamas, the good are supposed to either pass through a term of enjoyment in a region midway between the earth and the heaven, or the bad to undergo their measure of punishment in the nether world. After this time they return to Earth to animate new bodies. The good spirits can incarnated into human beings, and the best ones can ascend to heaven.

十殿阎君即十殿阎王，是中国特有的阎王系统，十殿阎王各有其职权，有司职人间寿夭生死，统管幽冥吉凶，有较人之善恶功过，接引超生，处罚罪鬼等。在中国民间阎王的知名度很高，民间大都认为人死后灵魂要受阎王审问，善多恶少者，仍可投胎做人；恶多善少者，发配地狱受苦；大善之人可升天做仙。

The Yamas in Ten Halls (selecte), by an unknown author, South Song dynasty

十殿阎君之一　南宋（1127—1279）

63

Chapter XXVIII

Learn to be hard as man

and remain soft as woman

like a stream in the world.

This stream in the world

will not depart from the way of virtue

but rejuvenate to its infancy.

Learn to be bright

and remain in the dark,

and try to be a model for the world.

A model for the world

will not stray from the way of virtue

but stretch to infinity.

dì èr shí bā zhāng
第 二 十 八 章

zhī qí xióng
知 其 雄,

shǒu qí cí
守 其 雌,

wéi tiān xià xī
为 天 下 溪。

wéi tiān xià xī
为 天 下 溪,

cháng dé bù lí
常 德 不 离,

fù guī yú yīng ér
复 归 于 婴 儿。

zhī qí bái
知 其 白,

shǒu qí hēi
守 其 黑,

wéi tiān xià shì
为 天 下 式。

wéi tiān xià shì
为 天 下 式,

cháng dé bù tè
常 德 不 忒,

fù guī yú wú jí
复 归 于 无 极。

The two hermits are enjoying the mountain views by the brook. The dense forest, the droopy vines and the running water give out charms of simplicity and lightness. Although the characters are very small, they are vivid in their forms and mind, are prominent for their elegance and transcendence. It looks like the wonder land which were aspired after by the nobles and literati in old times of China.

画中两位高士临溪眺望远处群山。山中林木繁茂，藤萝倒挂。山下一条大河，从左至右，奔流不息。图中山石林木，简淡有韵，人物虽小形神兼备，高雅脱俗，此景颇似洞天仙地，是中国古代文人仕大夫所心往之圣景及闲舒之生活愿景。

View Enjoying by the Brook, by Hua Yan, Qing dynasty

临泉轻眺图　华岩　清代

65

Learn to be glorious

and remain humble

like a vale in the world.

A vale in the world

will be fulfilled with constant virtue

and return to simplicity.

Simplicity may be diversified into instruments.

When a sage uses the instruments,

he becomes the ruler.

There should be unity in the rule of the great

sage.

zhī qí róng
知 其 荣，

shǒu qí rǔ
守 其 辱，

wéi tiān xià gǔ
为 天 下 谷。

wéi tiān xià gǔ
为 天 下 谷，

cháng dé nǎi zú
常 德 乃 足，

fù guī yú pǔ
复 归 于 朴。

pǔ sàn zé wéi qì
朴 散 则 为 器，

shèng rén yòng zhī
圣 人 用 之

zé wéi guān cháng
则 为 官 长。

gù dà zhì bù gē
故 大 制 不 割。

According to Daoism, as the ruler of the Earth and Heaven, Jade Emperor often makes his rounds to learn about the situations. Every time when he goes out, there must be a grand band of deities escorting him. This is a scene of the procession, among whom there are gods of Uranus and Big Dipper.

道教认为，人神之主的玉皇大帝为体察天上人间的实情，出跸巡视，有众神扈跸而行。本图就是众神随圣行跸的一个场景，图中有天皇、紫微等神仙。

The Escort by Deities, unknown author, Qing dynasty

众神扈跸　清代

Chapter XXIX

If anyone tries to take the world by force

and interfere with it,

I do not think he can succeed.

The world is a sacred realm

not to be interfered in.

Anyone who interferes in it will fail,

and who tries to keep it will lost it.

For things may lead or follow,

blow high or low,

be strong or weak,

loaded or unloaded.

So the sage will not go to excess,

to extravagance and to extreme.

dì èr shí jiǔ zhāng
第 二 十 九 章

jiāng yù qǔ tiān xià
将 欲 取 天 下

ér wéi zhī
而 为 之,

wú jiàn qí bù dé yǐ
吾 见 其 不 得 已。

tiān xià shén qì
天 下 神 器,

bù kě wéi yě
不 可 为 也,

wéi zhě bài zhī
为 者 败 之,

zhí zhě shī zhī
执 者 失 之。

gù wù huò xíng huò suí
故 物 或 行 或 随,

huò xū huò chuī
或 嘘 或 吹,

huò qiáng huò léi
或 强 或 羸,

huò zài huò zhuì
或 载 或 坠。

shì yǐ shèng rén qù shèn
是 以 圣 人 去 甚,

qù shē qù tài
去 奢 去 泰。

The character gets dressed in shabby clothes without sleeves and bosom, open his round eyes widely, wears a bottle gourd on his waist, stands in the water on bare feet and polishes his sword on a stone. We can also see an iron crutch lying in the water. The stream is completely limpid, meandering away among craggy stones. Some branches of old pines droop from above in the background. All things are dimly discernible in the cloud and mist. It looks like a new illustration to Iron-Crutch Li.

画中人物衣衫褴褛，圆睁大眼，袒胸露臂，腰挂一葫芦，赤足立于水中。他双手持宝剑，在巨石上磨砺，一拐杖旁置。脚下江水清澈见底，蜿蜒流淌，后面苍松半露倒垂，云雾飘渺，人物形象似八仙之一铁拐李。

The Sword Polishing on Stone, by Huang Ji, Ming dynasty

石磨剑图　黄济　明代

69

Chapter XXX

Those who follow the divine law to serve the ruler

will not conquer the world by force.

Conquerors will be conquered in turn.

Where goes the army,

there grow briars and thorns.

After a great war

comes a year of famine.

It is better to achieve good results

than to conquer by force.

Good results never lead to self-conceit,

nor to vain glory,

nor to undue pride.

Good results are something unavoidable,

not achieved by force.

The prime is followed by decline,

or it is against the divine law.

What is against the divine law will end early.

dì sān shí zhāng
第 三 十 章

yǐ dào zuǒ rén zhǔ zhě
以 道 佐 人 主 者,

bù yǐ bīng qiáng tián xià
不 以 兵 强 天 下。

qí shì hào huái
其 事 好 还。

shī zhī suǒ chǔ
师 之 所 处,

jīng jí shēng yān
荆 棘 生 焉。

dà jūn zhī hòu
大 军 之 后,

bì yǒu xiōng nián
必 有 凶 年。

shàn yǒu guǒ ér yǐ
善 有 果 而 已,

bù gǎn yǐ qǔ qiáng
不 敢 以 取 强。

guǒ ér wù jīn
果 而 勿 矜。

guǒ ér wù fá
果 而 勿 伐。

guǒ ér wù jiāo
果 而 勿 骄。

guǒ ér bù dé yǐ
果 而 不 得 已。

guǒ ér wù qiáng
果 而 勿 强。

wù zhuàng zé lǎo
物 壮 则 老,

shì wèi bù dào
是 谓 不 道,

bù dào zǎo yǐ
不 道 早 已。

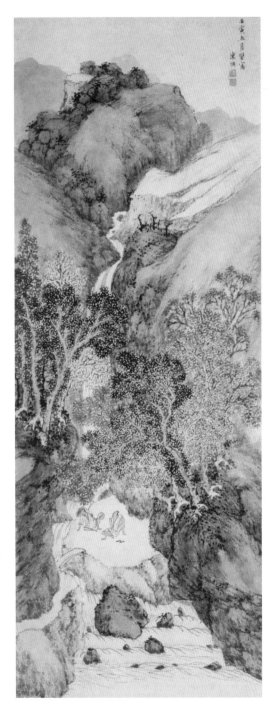

The ancient Chinese often drew analogy between water and Dao. In the picture, a brook is flying over down from the cliff along the deep valley and under the wood; two hermits are listening to the waterfall. The two characters are painted in free style, with vivid manners.

古人常用"水"来比喻"道"，本图描绘仙泉一泄直下，时隐时现于茂林深谷中，山下二高士驻足神会观象听瀑，人物意笔写之，神气十足。

Watching the Stream in the Wood, by Chen Huan, Ming dynasty

林溪观象图　陈焕　明代

Chapter XXXI

Weapons are tools of evil omen,

detested by all.

Those who follow the divine law will not

resort to them.

A worthy man prefers the left in time of

peace

and the right in time of war.

Weapons are tools of evil omen

not to be used by worthy men.

When they are compelled to use them,

the less often, the better.

Victory should not be glorified.

To glorify it

is to take delight in killing.

dì sān shí yī zhāng
第 三 十 一 章

fú bīng zhě bù xiáng zhī qì
夫 兵 者 不 祥 之 器,

wù huò wù zhī
物 或 恶 之,

gù yǒu dào zhě bù chù
故 有 道 者 不 处。

jūn zǐ jū zé guì zuǒ
君 子 居 则 贵 左,

yòng bīng zé guì yòu
用 兵 则 贵 右。

bīng zhě bù xiáng zhī qì
兵 者 不 祥 之 器,

fēi jūn zǐ zhī qì
非 君 子 之 器。

bù dé yǐ ér yòng zhī
不 得 已 而 用 之,

tián dàn wéi shàng
恬 淡 为 上。

shèng ér bù měi
胜 而 不 美,

ér měi zhī zhě
而 美 之 者,

shì lè shā rén
是 乐 杀 人。

Immortals, by an unknown author

仙人图

In Daoism, it is believed that people can transformed into immortals by persistent cultivation. These are four immortals secluding in the forest. Their ages are different which signify the different levels of cultivations.

道教重视今生，相信人坚持修炼，可以成为"仙人"，逍遥不死。图为描绘隐居山林的四位仙人，年龄高下不等，代表修仙品位上的差异。

Those delighted in killing

cannot do what they will in the world.

Good omen keeps to the left,

and evil omen to the right.

A lieutenant general keeps to the left,

and a full general to the right

as in the funeral service.

The heavier the casualties,

the deeper the mourning should be.

Even a victory should be celebrated

in funeral ceremony.

夫 乐 杀 人 者，

则 不 可 得 志 于 天 下 矣。

吉 事 尚 左，

凶 事 尚 右。

偏 将 军 居 左，

上 将 军 居 右。

言 以 丧 礼 处 之。

杀 人 之 众，

以 哀 悲 泣 之。

战 胜，

以 丧 礼 处 之。

The God of Thunder, selected from frescos in Yongle Palace, Yuan dynasty

雷公　永乐宫壁画(局部)　元代

It is the god whose duty is on thunder. It is believed in Daoism that the God of Thunder can present on behalf of the Heaven; he dominates blessings and disasters, determine people's death, therefore punishes the criminals.

道教中司雷击之神。道教认为雷霆可以为天代言；主天之灾福；司生死大权，用雷击惩凶除恶。

Chapter XXXII

The divine law is changeless,

it is nameless simplicity.

No matter how litter and simple,

the world cannot subdue it.

If rulers can observe it,

everything will be subject to their rule.

When heaven and earth mingle,

sweet dew will fall.

Not ordered by people,

it falls without prejudice.

When things begin to be named,

names come into being.

The beginning implies the end；

to know the end is to avoid danger.

The divine law will prevail in the world

just as streams flow from the vale to

the river and the sea.

dì sān shí èr zhāng
第 三 十 二 章

dào cháng
道 常，

wú míng zhī pǔ
无 名 之 朴。

suī xiǎo
虽 小，

tiān xià mò néng chén
天 下 莫 能 臣。

hóu wáng ruò néng shǒu zhī
侯 王 若 能 守 之，

wàn wù jiàng zì bīn
万 物 将 自 宾。

tiān dì xiāng hé
天 地 相 合，

yǐ jiàng gān lù
以 降 甘 露，

mín mò zhī lìng
民 莫 之 令

ér zì jūn
而 自 均。

shǐ zhì yǒu míng
始 制 有 名，

míng yì jì yǒu
名 亦 既 有，

fū yì jiàng zhī zhǐ
夫 亦 将 知 止，

zhī zhǐ kě yǐ bù dài
知 止 可 以 不 殆。

pì dào zhī zài tiān xià
譬 道 之 在 天 下，

yóu chuān gǔ zhī yú jiāng hǎi
犹 川 谷 之 于 江 海。

A hermit is walking with a cane in his hand among the plum trees and watching delightedly his attendant dancing with the crane. The flowers and trees grow quietly in the remote valley, and the faraway mountains stand in the clouds. The pattern and style of the painting are ethereal and primitive with numinous touches.

图绘一隐士拄杖游憩于一片梅林之中，笑看书童与仙鹤相向对舞。坡下幽林曲径，远处山峦连绵，飘渺如黛，隐没于云中。意境虚空旷朗，格调高古洒脱。

Being with the Crane and Plums, by Hua Yan, Qing dynasty

梅鹤图　华岩　清代

Chapter XXXIII

It needs observation to know others,

but reflection to konw oneself.

Physically strong, one can conquer others；

mentally strong, one can couquer oneself.

Content, one is rich；

with strong will, one can persevere.

Staying where one should, one can endure

long；

Unforgettable, one is immortal.

dì sān shí sān zhāng
第 三 十 三 章

zhī rén zhě zhì
知 人 者 智,
zì zhī zhě míng
自 知 者 明。
shèng rén zhě yǒu lì
胜 人 者 有 力,
zì shèng zhě qiáng
自 胜 者 强。
zhī zú zhě fù
知 足 者 富,
qiáng xíng zhě yǒu zhì
强 行 者 有 志。
bù shī qí suǒ zhě jiǔ
不 失 其 所 者 久,
sǐ ér bù wáng zhě shòu
死 而 不 亡 者 寿。

Doumu is the name for the Mother of Big Dipper. She is a goddess who controls not only the natural process of heaven and earth, ying and yang, e.g. wind, rain, thunder, and lightening, etc, but also the social changes, e.g., fertility, longevity, filialness, exploits and profits. The three eyes of her image represent the heaven, earth and human beings; the four heads represent the four Lunar Mansions, e.g. the Green Dragon in the East, the White Tiger in the West, the Red Phoenix in the South and the Black Turtle-Snake in the North; the eight arms represent the four sides and the four coigns. The Sun and the Moon on the hands symbolize the heaven and the earth, and the bell the wind, the sword the rainbow, the stamp the thunder, the spear the meteor, the two hands with clutching fingers stand for the Big Dipper surrounded by all stars.

斗母元君，又称"斗母"、斗姥、斗姆、中天梵炁斗母元君，北斗九真圣德天后。斗姆是道教信奉的女神，道经称"斗姆乃北斗众星之母"。虽相貌奇特，但面现慈容。

The Original Lady of Doumu, by an unknown author, Ming dynasty

斗母元君　明代

Chapter XXXIV

The divine law is a stream

overflowing letf and right.

All things grow from it,

and it never turns away.

It achieves the deed without the fame.

It breeds all thing

but will not claim to be their lord.

So it may be called "Little."

All things cling to it,

but it will not claim to be their master.

So it may be called "Great."

As it never claims to be great,

so it becomes great.

dì sān shí sì zhāng
第 三 十 四 章

dà dào fàn xi
大 道 泛 兮,

qí kě zuǒ yòu
其 可 左 右。

wàn wù shì zhī yǐ shēng
万 物 恃 之 以 生

ér bù cí
而 不 辞,

gōng chéng ér bù míng yǒu
功 成 而 不 名 有,

yī yǎng wàn wù
衣 养 万 物

ér bù wéi zhǔ
而 不 为 主。

kě míng yú xiǎo
可 名 于 小;

wàn wù gui yān
万 物 归 焉

ér bù wéi zhǔ
而 不 为 主,

kě míng wéi dà
可 名 为 大。

yǐ qí zhōng bù zì wéi dà
以 其 终 不 自 为 大,

gù néng chéng qí dà
故 能 成 其 大。

Ge Zhichuan (284-364, also known as Ge Hong) is best known for his interest in Daoism, alchemy, and techniques of longevity. He and his family moved to Mount Luofu (now in Guangdong) to be a local official when he learned that there was a lot ores for alchemical use. This picture illustrates this story. The characters are simple and natural, the cliffs are steep and high, benefiting the whole vision with profound meanings.

此画描绘了晋代名士葛稚川携家人移居罗浮山的情景。人物形象古朴自然，山石林立，峻岭重重，意境幽远。

Ge Zhichuan's Family Moving to Mount Luofu, by Wang Meng, Yuan dynasty

葛稚川移居图 王蒙 元代

Chapter XXXV

Keeping the great image in mind,

you may go everywhere.

Wherever you go, you bring no harm

but safety, peace and security.

Music and food

may attract travellers.

The divine law is tasteless

when it comes out of the mouth.

It is invisible when looked at,

inaudible when listened to,

and inexhaustible when used.

dì sān shí wǔ zhāng
第 三 十 五 章

zhí dà xiàng
执 大 象,

tiān xià wǎng
天 下 往。

wǎng ér bù hài
往 而 不 害,

ān píng tài
安 平 泰。

lè yǔ ěr
乐 与 饵,

guò kè zhǐ
过 客 止。

dào zhī chū kǒu
道 之 出 口,

dàn hū qí wú wèi
淡 乎 其 无 味。

shì zhī bù zú jiàn
视 之 不 足 见,

tīng zhī bù zú wén
听 之 不 足 闻,

yòng zhī bù zú jì
用 之 不 足 既。

An old man is sitting leisurely on a rock by the brook bank and under a pine tree with his hand resting on the knee, and looking up to distance concentratedly and thoughtfully. With the background of a standing attendant, the huge pine tree, some branches of bamboos and a lot of remote cliffs and mountains, the painting has been given with a light, ethereal quality that reminds people of an immortal world. The pine tree also signifies longevity and the mountain great success.

画中老者闲坐水边松下石台
上，一手抚膝，仰首远眺，神
情安然专注，若有所思，旁立
一童，松涛掩映之处，群峰叠
立，疏竹临溪，好似神仙之轻
松惬意。也寓意"如松柏之寿，
如嵩山之禄。"

The Songs in Forest, by Ma Yuan, South Song dynasty

松涛图　马远　南宋

83

Chapter XXXVI

Inhale

before you exhale!

Strengthen

what is to be weakened!

Raise

what is to fall!

Give

before you take!

Such is the twilight before the day.

The soft and weak may overcome the

hard and strong.

Fish should not go out of deep water.

The sharpest weapon of a state

should not be shown to others.

jiāng yù xī zhī
将 欲 歙 之,

bì gù zhāng zhī
必 固 张 之。

jiāng yù ruò zhī
将 欲 弱 之,

bì gù qiáng zhī
必 固 强 之。

jiāng yù fèi zhī
将 欲 废 之,

bì gù xīng zhī
必 固 兴 之。

jiāng yù qǔ zhī
将 欲 取 之,

bì gù yǔ zhī
必 固 与 之。

shì wèi wēi míng
是 谓 微 明。

róu ruò shèng gāng qiáng
柔 弱 胜 刚 强,

yú bù kě tuō yú yuān
鱼 不 可 脱 于 渊。

guó zhī lì qì
国 之 利 器,

bù kě yǐ shì rén
不 可 以 示 人。

The Constellation of Longevity (selected), by Lü Ji, Ming dynasty

寿星图(局部)　吕纪　明代

The Constellation of Longevity is also called the Great Emperor of Longevity of the South Pole. His duty is to manage people's life spans. He has been listed among the gods enjoying the imperial worship since Qin dynasty. Therefore he is quite loved by people and a popular character of painting in traditional China. He was usually portrayed as having a lumpy forehead, white hair and beard, and generally appearing as a gentle and happy old man holding a gnarled cane. But this picture has shifted to a more vivid episode. The deer as a symbol of long life is listening to perhaps the words of the constellation or the sound of the brook.

道教追求修练成仙，因而其神系中有一位主掌人寿命的天神就是寿星，又称南极仙翁，南极真君。历代画家皆喜绘画寿星形象，本图寿星形象质朴可爱，旁有一小鹿歪头凝视，石下清泉有声，是寿星画中的杰作。

Chapter XXXVII

The divine law will not interfere,

so there is nothing it cannot do.

If rulers can follow it,

everything will be done by itself.

If there is desire to do anything,

I shall control it

with nameless simplicity.

When controlled by nameless

simplicity,

there will be no desire.

Without desire, there will be tranquillity,

and the world will be peaceful by itself.

dì sān shí qī zhāng
第 三 十 七 章

dào cháng wú wéi
道 常 无 为,

ér wú bù wéi
而 无 不 为。

hóu wáng ruò néng shǒu zhī
侯 王 若 能 守 之,

wàn wù jiāng zì huà
万 物 将 自 化。

huà ér yù zuò
化 而 欲 作,

wú jiāng zhèn zhī
吾 将 镇 之

yǐ wú míng zhī pǔ
以 无 名 之 朴。

zhèn zhī yǐ
镇 之 以,

wú míng zhī pǔ
无 名 之 朴,

fū yì jiāng wú yù
夫 亦 将 无 欲。

bù yù yǐ jìng
不 欲 以 静,

tiān xià jiāng zì dìng
天 下 将 自 定。

He is the lord of thunder ministry of the Heavenly Court. He lives in the highest level of heaven, in charge of five courts, which are courts of the heavenly thunder, earthly thunder, water thunder, spiritual thunder and territorial thunder, and three bureaus, which is the bureau of ten thousand thunders, thunderbolts and thunder judgments.

全称为"九天应元雷声普化天尊"。《灵宝领教济度全书》称：尊属九天之上，宗司五雷（天雷、地雷、水雷、神雷、社雷）应化九天，总管雷霆都府、辖及二院（五雷院、驱邪院、）三司（万神雷司、雷霆都司、雷霆部司），为雷部尊神。

The God of Thunder and his Generals, by an unknown author, Ming dynasty

雷声普化天尊及诸天将　明代

Chapter XXXVIII

A man of high virtue does not claim

he has virtue,

so he is virtuous.

A man of low virtue claims he has not

lost virtue,

so he is virtueless.

A man of high virtue does nothing on

purpose；

a man of low virtue does nothing

without purpose.

A good man does good without

purpose；

a just man does good on purpose.

When a formalist does good without

receiving response,

dì sān shí bā zhāng
第 三 十 八 章

shàng dé bù dé
上 德 不 德，

shì yǐ yǒu dé
是 以 有 德。

xià dé bù shī dé
下 德 不 失 德，

shì yǐ wú dé
是 以 无 德。

shàng dé wú wéi ér wú yǐ wéi
上 德 无 为，而 无 以 为；

xià dé wú wéi ér yǒu yǐ wéi
下 德 无 为，而 有 以 为。

shàng rén wéi zhī ér wú yǐ wéi
上 仁 为 之，而 无 以 为；

shàng yì wéi zhī ér yǒu yǐ wéi
上 义 为 之，而 有 以 为。

shàng lǐ wéi zhī ér mò zhī yìng
上 礼 为 之，而 莫 之 应，

zé rǎng bì ér rēng zhī
则 攘 臂 而 扔 之。

gù shī dào ér hòu dé
故 失 道 而 后 德，

shī dé ér hòu rén
失 德 而 后 仁，

He is one of the Eight Immortals. He lived as an occult master on Mount Zhongtiao in Heng Prefecture during the Tang Dynasty. By the time of Empress Wu (684~705), he claimed to be several hundred years old. Empress Wu summoned him to leave the mountain, so he feigned death. However until Emperor Xuanzong(reigining from 712 to 756) he was still alive because the emperor was recorded giving him an official titles. He is the personification of a white bat. He rides a white donkey backward, carries a phoenix-feather or a peach of immortality. In this picture, the peaches, flowers, fairy maidens, bamboos, gnarled canes and the white crane are all preferred symbols of immortality which signify a lot of meanings.

石壁悬生蟠桃一树,垂实累累。树下张果老及二仙女,一添香宝鼎,一执如意侍立。白鹤憩游于竹林,紫芝傍生于石隙。张果老为八仙之一, 原为唐代道士,常隐居恒州中条山,往来汾、晋之间,相传年寿数百岁,尊称为张果老。民间传说的形象是背负道情筒, 倒骑白驴, 云游四方, 劝化世人。

Zhang Guolao, by an unknown author, Song Dynasty

果老仙踪图　宋代

he will stretch out his arms to enforce

compliance.

So virtue is lost when the divine law

is not followed;

humanism is lost after virtue;

justice is lost after humanism;

formalism is lost after justice.

Formalism show the gradual loss of

loyalty and faith,

and the beginning of disorder.

Foresight is the superfluous

part of the divine low,

leading to ignorance.

Therefore a true great man

prefers the thick to the thin,

the substantial to the superfluos.

He rejects not the former but the latter.

shī rén ér hòu yì
失 仁 而 后 义，

shī yì ér hòu lǐ
失 义 而 后 礼。

fū lǐ zhě
夫 礼 者，

zhōng xìn zhī bó
忠 信 之 薄，

ér luàn zhī shǒu
而 乱 之 首；

qián shí zhě
前 识 者，

dào zhī huá
道 之 华，

ér yú zhī shǐ
而 愚 之 始。

shì yǐ dà zhàng fū chǔ qí hòu
是 以 大 丈 夫 处 其 厚，

bù jū qí bó
不 居 其 薄；

chǔ qí shí
处 其 实，

bù jū qí huá
不 居 其 华。

gù qù bǐ qǔ cǐ
故 去 彼 取 此。

The immortal lady is standing there with her palms holding together and with an aura surrounding her head. The fairy maiden is attending with a plate of peaches. To celebrate birthday with peaches is a routine image of the Queen Mother of the West, so it is supposed to be her. This portrait of the immortal lady is quite tender, graceful and beautiful.

此画中女仙合掌而立，头背有圆光，侍女捧盘献桃。献桃故事向与西王母关联，画中女仙当是西王母。民间习称王母娘娘。道教将西王母列为最高女神。造型上也为古代温雅美丽女性的象征。

Birthday's Gift, by an unknown author, Yuan dynasty

献寿图　元代

Chapter XXXIX

When one with the divine law,

heaven is clear,

earth is stable,

spirits are divine,

valleys are full,

all creatures are alive,

rulers are noble in the world.

Why are they one with the divine law?

If not clear, heaven would split；

if not stable, earth would quake；

if not divine, spirts would disappear；

if not full, valley would parch；

if not alive, all creatures would perish；

if not high and noble, rulers would fall.

dì sān shí jiǔ zhāng
第 三 十 九 章

xī zhī dé yī zhě
昔 之 得 一 者：

tiān dé yī yǐ qīng
天 得 一 以 清，

dì dé yī yǐ níng
地 得 一 以 宁，

shén dé yī yǐ líng
神 得 一 以 灵，

gǔ dé yī yǐ yíng
谷 得 一 以 盈，

wàn wù dé yī yǐ shēng
万 物 得 一 以 生，

hóu wáng dé yī yǐ wéi tiān xià guì
侯 王 得 一 以 为 天 下 贵。

qí zhì zhī
其 致 之，

tiān wú yǐ qīng jiāng kǒng liè
天 无 以 清 将 恐 裂，

dì wú yǐ níng jiāng kǒng fèi
地 无 以 宁 将 恐 废，

shén wú yǐ líng jiāng kǒng xiē
神 无 以 灵 将 恐 歇，

gǔ wú yǐ yíng jiāng kǒng jié
谷 无 以 盈 将 恐 竭，

wàn wù wú yǐ shēng jiāng kǒng miè
万 物 无 以 生 将 恐 灭，

hóu wáng wú yǐ guì jiāng kǒng jué
侯 王 无 以 贵 将 恐 蹶。

There are nine levels in the heaven in which Shenxiao or Empyrean is the highest, according to Daoism. There are nine gods who habitat on it: the God of Longevity, Green Flowers, Universalization, Thunder, Taiyi, Dongyuan, Liubo and Caifang. They are born from the primordial Qi and in charge of the creation and maintenance.

道教认为：天有九霄，而神霄为最高。神霄之上，有神霄九宸上帝，即长生大帝、青华大帝、普化天尊、雷神大帝、太乙天尊、洞渊大帝、六波帝君、采访真君等九位。《太清玉册》称："即元始九气化生也，故号九宸上帝，代天以司造化，主宰万灵。"

The Empyrean Gods, by an unknown author, Qing dynasty

神霄九宸上帝　清代

Thus the noble rely on the humble,

and the high is based on the low.

That is why rulers call themselves sole

and unworthy.

Do they not rely on the humble as their

base?

Is it not ture?

Therefore, too much honor amounts to

no honor.

We should have no desire for glittering

jade

nor for tinkling stone.

gù guì yǐ jiàn wéi běn
故 贵 以 贱 为 本,

gāo yǐ xià wéi jī
高 以 下 为 基。

shì yǐ hóu wáng zì chēng gū guǎ bù gǔ
是 以 侯 王 自 称 孤 寡 不 毂。

cǐ fēi yǐ jiàn wéi běn yé
此 非 以 贱 为 本 耶?

fēi hū
非 乎?

gù zhì yù wú yù
故 至 誉 无 誉。

bù yù lù lù rú yù
不 欲 璐 璐 如 玉,

luò luò rú shí
珞 珞 如 石。

Chapter XL

dì sì shí zhāng
第 四 十 章

The divine law may go opposite ways;

even weakness is useful.

All things in the world come into being

with a form;

the form comes form the formless.

fǎn zhě
反 者,

dào zhī dòng
道 之 动;

ruò zhě
弱 者,

dào zhī yòng
道 之 用。

tiān xià wàn wù shēng yú yǒu
天 下 万 物 生 于 有,

yǒu shēng yú wú
有 生 于 无。

The God of Village have developed from land worship. Before Gods of Towns dominated in China, land worship had a hierarchy of deities conforming strictly to social structure, in which the emperor, kings, dukes, officials and common people were allowed to worship only the land gods within their command; the highest land deity was the Earthly Queen of the Four Imperial Ones. Ranked lower than Town Gods, the God of Village have been very popular among villagers as the grassroot deities since the 14th century during the Ming Dynasty. Some scholars speculate that this change came because of a royal edict, because it is reported that the first emperor of the Ming dynasty was born in a Village God shrine. The image of the Village God is that of a simply clothed, smiling, white-bearded man. His wife, the Grandma of the Village, looks like any old lady who lives next door.

土地又称"社公"、"土地爷"。土地神的信仰，来源于古代的"社神"崇拜。旧俗以土地为民众继嗣之神，以求年岁丰登，地方平安。道教斋醮法坛，礼请诸神，醮事圆满之后，由土地送回诸神，又称"送圣土地"。

The God of Villages, by an unknown author, Qing dynasty

土地　清代

95

Chapter XLI

Having heard the divine law,

a good scholar follows it;

a common scholar

half believes in it;

a poor schcolar laughs at it.

If not laughed at, it cannot be the divine

law.

Therefore it is said

the way to light seems dark;

the forward way seems to go backward;

the smooth way seems rough.

So high virtue looks like low vale,

infinite virtue seems insufficient,

established virtue seems boorrowed,

simplicity seems clumsy.

So purity seems soiled,

dì sì shí yī zhāng
第 四 十 一 章

shàng shì swén dào
上 士 闻 道,

qín ér xíng zhī
勤 而 行 之;

zhōng shì wén dào
中 士 闻 道,

ruò cún ruò wáng
若 存 若 亡;

xià shì wén dào dà xiào zhī
下 士 闻 道 大 笑 之,

bù xiào bù zú yǐ wéi dào
不 笑 不 足 以 为 道。

gù jiàn yán yǒu zhī
故 建 言 有 之:

míng dào ruò mèi
明 道 若 昧,

jìn dào ruò tuì
进 道 若 退,

yí dào ruò lèi
夷 道 若 类。

shàng dé ruò gǔ
上 德 若 谷,

guǎng dé ruò bù zú
广 德 若 不 足,

In Daoism, she is the ruler of the western paradise, the head of the goddesses and goddess of immortality. Originally she was a ferocious goddess with the teeth of a tiger, who sent plagues down upon the world. After she was adopted into the Daoist pantheon, she was transformed into a benign deity. Her role with respect to immortality and everlasting happiness probably arose from her origin as the goddess of fertility. On the third day of March every year on Lunar Calendar, Daoists celebrate his birthday. According to legends, on that day deities all go to join her birthday party. In rewards, she hosts a grand banquet of peaches for the guests in her Jade Palace (yao chi).

王母，即"西王母"，俗称"王母娘娘"，是天上职位最高的一位女性神仙，所有得道成仙的女子都隶属于她。相传农历三月初三为王母圣诞，是日群仙皆来为之庆寿，王母在其所居瑶池蟠桃园，设宴会，酬谢群仙。

The Queen Mother of the West, by an unknown author, Qing dynasty

王母庆寿　清代

97

a large square seems cornerless,

a great vessel is the last completed,

a great sound is inaudible,

a great image is formless,

an invisible law is nameless.

Only the divine law is good from the

beginning to the end.

jiàn dé ruò tōu
建 德 若 偷，

zhì zhēn ruò yú
质 真 若 渝，

dà bái ruò rǔ
大 白 若 辱，

dà fāng wú yú
大 方 无 隅，

dà qì wǎn chéng
大 器 晚 成，

dà yīn xī shēng
大 音 希 声，

dà xiàng wú xíng
大 象 无 形，

dào yǐn wú míng
道 隐 无 名。

fú wéi dào shàn shǐ qiě shàn chéng
夫 惟 道 善 始 且 善 成。

Dragon King's Palace, by an unknown author, Yuan dynasty

龙宫水府图　无款　元代

The palace is visible through huge waves with a magnificent spectacle. The Dragon King attended by fairy maidens and ministers is making an interview with a governmental official who is also attended with a guard and a horse. It is really a gorgeous imagination.

图绘惊涛骇浪中龙宫显现，富丽堂皇。龙王在侍女、神将的簇拥下接见一官人，侍者牵马傍立。

Chapter XLII

One is the child of the divine law.

After one come two,

after two come three,

after three come all things.

Everything has a bright and a dark side,

co-existent in harmony.

People dislike to be

lonely and worthless.

But rulers call themselves the sole and

unworthy.

So things may gain when they seem to

lose,

or lose when they seem to gain.

I will teach

what others teach me.

The brute will die a brutal death.

I will teach this as a lesson.

dì sì shí èr zhāng
第四十二章

dào shēng yī
道 生 一，

yī shēng èr
一 生 二，

èr shēng sān
二 生 三，

sān shēng wàn wù
三 生 万 物。

wàn wù fù yīn ér bào yáng
万 物 负 阴 而 抱 阳，

chōng qì yǐ wéi hé
冲 气 以 为 和。

rén zhī suǒ wù
人 之 所 恶，

wéi gū guǎ bù gǔ
唯 孤 寡 不 毂，

ér wáng gōng yǐ wéi chēng
而 王 公 以 为 称。

gù wù huò sǔn zhī ér yì
故 物 或 损 之 而 益，

huò yì zhī ér sǔn
或 益 之 而 损。

rén zhī suǒ jiào
人 之 所 教，

wǒ yì jiào zhī
我 亦 教 之，

qiáng liáng zhě bù dé qí sǐ
强 梁 者 不 得 其 死，

wǔ jiāng yǐ wéi jiào fù
吾 将 以 为 教 父。

Zhaijiao Liturgy, by an unknown author

斋醮科仪图

Zhaijiao Liturgy is a kind of Daoist ceremony. This is a depiction of one procedure of it.

图中反映道士在做法事。高功在主持法事。

Chapter XLIII

The softest thing in the world

can penetrate the hardest.

There is no space but the matterless can enter.

Thus I see

the utility of doing nothing.

The teaching by saying nothing

and the utility of doing nothing

are seldom known to the world.

dì sì shí sān zhāng
第 四 十 三 章

tiān xià zhī zhì róu
天 下 之 至 柔,

chí chěng tiān xià zhī zhì jiān
驰 骋 天 下 之 至 坚,

wú yǒu rù wú jiān
无 有 入 无 间。

wú shì yǐ zhī
吾 是 以 知

wú wéi zhī yǒu yì
无 为 之 有 益。

bù yán zhī jiào
不 言 之 教,

wú wéi zhī yì
无 为 之 益,

tiān xià xī jí zhī
天 下 希 及 之。

Chapter XLIV

Which do you love better, fame or life?

Which do you like more, health or wealth?

Which will do you more harm, gain or loss?

The more you love, the more you spend.

The more you store up, the more you lose.

As a result, contentment brings no shame；

knowledge of the limit brings no danger.

Thus you can be safe for long.

dì sì shí sì zhāng
第 四 十 四 章

míng yǔ shēn shú qīn
名 与 身 孰 亲?

shēn yǔ huò shú duō
身 与 货 孰 多?

dé yǔ wáng shú bìng
得 与 亡 孰 病?

shì gù shèn ài bì dà fèi
是 故, 甚 爱 必 大 费,

duō cáng bì hòu wáng
多 藏 必 厚 亡。

zhī zú bù rǔ
知 足 不 辱,

zhī zhǐ bù dài
知 止 不 殆,

kě yǐ cháng jiǔ
可 以 长 久。

He is the divine guardian of Daoism. He was named Wangshan when he was a historical figure during the reign of Emperor Huizong of the Song Dynasty. He was originally a safeguard of the Jade Emperor's Sacred Heaven Palace, appointed by Jade Emperor to be the Town God of Huaiyin Prefecture in Jiangsu Province. One day, when the Perfected Mater Sa passed by the temple of Wang, the local governor drove him away under the request of Wang. Sa was shamed and furious, and burnt Wang's temple using magic, making Wang homeless. Wang had no choice but followed Sa for more than 10 years as a subordinate. In Ming dynasty, Wang was royally laurelled as a god. Since then, Wangshan has become the Guardian God in the first hall of Daoist temples, and has been honored as Divine General Wang.

王灵官神是道教护法神将，又称火车灵官王元帅，纠察天上人间，除邪祛恶，卫护正法。

The Divine General Wang, by an unknown author, Ming dynasty

王灵官神　明代

103

Chapter XLV

Perfection does not seem flawless,

but it can be used for long.

What is full still has vacancy,

but it can be used endlessly.

The straight may seem crooked；

the most skillful may seem clumsy；

the most eloquent may seem slow of

speech.

Be calm rather than rash；

be cool rather than hot.

Serenity is the right way in the world.

dì sì shí wǔ zhāng
第 四 十 五 章

dà chéng ruò quē
大 成 若 缺，

qí yòng bù bì
其 用 不 弊，

dà yíng ruò chōng
大 盈 若 冲，

qí yòng bù qióng
其 用 不 穷。

dà zhí ruò qū
大 直 若 屈，

dà qiǎo ruò zhuó
大 巧 若 拙，

dà biàn ruò nè
大 辩 若 讷。

jìng shèng zào
静 胜 躁，

hán shèng rè
寒 胜 热。

qīng jìng wéi tiān xià zhèng
清 静 为 天 下 正。

The Yellow Emperor Requesting Dao with Guangchengzi, by Wu Wei, Ming dynasty

黄帝向广成子问道图　吴伟　明代

The Yellow Emperor is believed to be the founder father of Chinese civilization. And Guangchengzi is a legendary Immortal who lived in a stone cave in Mt. Kongdong, now in Linru County, Henan Province. This is an illustration to the story happened between them. As recorded in Zhuangzi, when the Yellow Emperor heard that Master Guangcheng was living on top of Mount Kongdong. He therefore went to visit him. Guangchengzi told him what he has done and said is too shallow and greedy, and how he can be talked about Dao. The emperor withdrew, built a solitary hut and lived in it for three months in retirement. Then he went once more to request an interview. Guangchengzi thus taught him the arts of governing both of state and the body, such as that the essence of the perfect Dao is deep and darkly shrouded, and the ultimate of the perfect Dao is mysterious and hushed in silence. If you see nothing, hear nothing and keep calm with spirit within yourself, your body will correct itself. If your eyes see nothing, if your ears hear nothing and your heart knows nothing, your spirit will preserve your body, and your body will have a long life. Be cautious of your heart, and close your eyes to the outside. You will fail if you know too much. Since I have kept to Oneness and remained in peace, I have lived twelve hundred years without growing old. He also said that he who attains my Dao will be the emperor in Heaven above and King on Earth below; he who loses my Dao will see only light above and earth below. After saying goodbye to you, I go through the door of infinitude, and travel through endless realms. I will shine with the Sun and Moon, and will live eternally with Heaven and Earth.

　　黄帝乃华夏文明之始祖。此幅画卷反映了黄帝往崆峒山拜见广成子，向他叙述自己的企望和抱负，想取天地之精华以佐五谷的生长，想获得管阴阳的本领以利群生。广成子却告诫他，你要问的是事物的本质，而所追求的确是事物的渣滓，如此多欲，岂可谈道。黄帝听后甚为惊讶，退回后躲进静室斋戒三月，再往求道。广成子授黄帝《自然经》。

Chapter XLVI

When the world goes the right way,

battle steeds are used for tillage.

When the world goes the wrong way,

pregnant mares are used in war.

No crime is greater than insatiable desire；

no woe is greater than covetise.

If you know contentment comes from being

content,

you will always have enough.

dì   sì   shí   liù   zhāng
第 四 十 六 章

tiān   xià   yǒu   dào
天 下 有 道,

què   zǒu   mǎ   yǐ   fèn
却 走 马 以 粪。

tiān   xià   wú   dào
天 下 无 道,

róng   mǎ   shēng   yú   jiāo
戎 马 生 于 郊。

huò   mò   dà   yú   bù   zhī   zú
祸 莫 大 于 不 知 足;

jiù   mò   dà   yú   yù   dé
咎 莫 大 于 欲 得。

gù   zhī   zú   zhī   zú
故 知 足 之 足,

cháng   zú   yǐ
常 足 矣。

The Sacred Mountains of China are divided into two groups associated with Daoism and Buddhism. The Daoist ones are called "Sacred Abodes and Blessed Lands" (Dongtian Fudi), which have been important destinations for pilgrimage and immortal cultivations. This is a picture on one of the Daoist mountains. The peaks pierce through above the white clouds and therefore the temple's halls on the terrace among the peaks are hidden in the clouds and behind the old trees gleamingly. It is quite a sacred land secluded far away from the mundane world.

仙峰堂堂，白云萦绕，树木翁郁，
山路幽深，溪间映带，道观隐现，
正是道人居住的洞天福地。

The Remote Halls on the Sacred Mountains, by unknown author, Later Jin dynasty (936-947)

洞天山堂图　无款　金代

107

Chapter XLVII

You may know the outside world

without going out.

You may know the divine law

without looking out of the window.

The farther you go out.

the less you may learn.

Therefore the sage learns all.

without going far away.

He becomes well-known without looking out,

and accomplishes all without doing anything.

dì sì shí qī zhāng
第 四 十 七 章

bù chū hù
不 出 户,

zhī tiān xià
知 天 下;

bù kuī yǒu
不 窥 牖,

jiàn tiān dào
见 天 道。

qí chū mí yuǎn
其 出 弥 远,

qí zhī mí shǎo
其 知 弥 少。

shì yǐ shèng rén
是 以 圣 人

bù xíng ér zhī
不 行 而 知。

bù jiàn ér míng
不 见 而 名,

bù wéi ér chéng
不 为 而 成。

God of Town is a protector of towns and cities and is also an upholder of social justice. People believe that this deity is capable of effecting a snowy or rainy or sunny weather as it is entreated to do.In a Daoist ritual, this deity is often the one who receives the guest deities coming from outside its juridiction.

城隍原为古代守护城池之神，后为道教所信奉，《太上老君说城隍感应消灾保福妙经》称城隍为"剪恶除凶、护国保邦"之神，旱时降雨，涝时放晴，以保谷丰民足。道教斋醮法坛，礼请诸神，通过城隍迎请而至，又称"请圣城隍"。

The God of the Town, by an unknown author, Ming dynasty

城隍图 明代

Chapter XLVIII

The more you know of the human world,

the less you know of the divine law.

Less and less you need to know

till nothing need to be done.

When you need do nothing, there is

nothing you cannot do.

If you need do nothing,

then you can rule over the world.

If everything need you to do,

then you cannot rule over the world.

dì sì shí bā zhāng
第 四 十 八 章

wéi xué rì yì
为 学 日 益。

wéi dào rì sǔn
为 道 日 损。

sǔn zhī yòu sǔn
损 之 又 损,

yǐ zhì yú wú wéi
以 至 于 无 为。

wú wéi ér wú bù wéi
无 为 而 无 不 为。

qǔ tiān xià cháng yǐ wú shì
取 天 下 常 以 无 事,

jí qí yǒu shì
及 其 有 事,

bù zú yǐ qǔ tiān xià
不 足 以 取 天 下。

He is one of the four marshals under Divine General Wang. The other three marshals are Ma Cheng, Zhao Gongming and Yue Fei.

四大元帅，为王灵官手下的四位元帅，负责守护道观，巡查世间善恶。四帅为温琼、马晟、赵公明、岳飞四人。

Marshal Wen, by an unknown author, approximately from Song to Yuan dynasty

四帅之一的温元帅　南宋至元

Chapter XLIX

The sage has no personal will;

he takes the people's will as his own.

He is good not only to those who are good,

but also to those who are not,

so all become good.

He trusts not only the trustworthy,

but also those who are not,

so all become trustworthy.

The sage seems simple

in the world,

he simplifies all the people's mind.

The people are all eyes and ears;

the sage restores them to their childhood.

dì sì shí jiǔ zhāng
第 四 十 九 章

shèng rén wú cháng xīn
圣 人 无 常 心，

yǐ bǎi xìng xīn wéi xīn
以 百 姓 心 为 心。

shàn zhě wú shàn zhī
善 者 吾 善 之，

bū shàn zhě wú yì shàn zhī
不 善 者 吾 亦 善 之，

dé shàn
德 善。

xìn zhě wú xìn zhī
信 者 吾 信 之，

bū xìn zhě wú yì xìn zhī
不 信 者 吾 亦 信 之，

dé xìn
德 信。

shèng rén zài tiān xià
圣 人 在 天 下，

shè shè yān
歙 歙 焉，

wéi tiān xià hùn qí xīn
为 天 下 浑 其 心。

bǎi xìng jiē zhù qí ěr mù
百 姓 皆 注 其 耳 目，

shèng rén jiē hái zhī
圣 人 皆 孩 之。

It was told that the immortals take extraordinary diet such as some powerful fungi and minerals instead of household foods. Fungus is believed to have divine power of longevity and healing. This picture illustrates this kind of ideas. The immortal is picking up his diet in the mountain. The huge peach in his hand, fungi in his pannier and the crane behind him, are all the ideal objects for the cultivating consumption.

传说中仙人的生活，"食则翠芝朱英"。求长生不死的灵药，芝是最为重要的一种。采芝的题材也就相当常见。本幅画仙人手捧大桃，肩荷锄挂药篮，篮中有紫芝，一鹤随后。

An Immortal Picking Up Fungi, by Wang Qihan, Later Tang (923-936)

采芝仙　王齐翰　五代南唐

113

Chapter L

From birth to death,

one-third of men live long,

one-third die early,

and one-third

live and move

near the realm of death.

How can it be so?

For men overvalue a long life.

In fact, those who live long

will not go near rhinos or tigers

on land,

nor go to war in armor with shield,

so that rhinos have no use of their

horns,

and tigers of their claws,

and soldiers of their swords.

How can it be so?

For they will not come near the

realm of death.

dì wǔ shí zhāng
第 五 十 章

chū shēng rù sǐ
出 生 入 死，

shēng zhī tú shí yǒu sān
生 之 徒 十 有 三，

sǐ zhī tú shí yǒu sān
死 之 徒 十 有 三。

rén zhī shēng
人 之 生，

dòng zhī yú sǐ dì
动 之 于 死 地，

yì shí yǒu sān
亦 十 有 三。

fū hé gù
夫 何 故？

yǐ qí shēng shēng zhī hòu
以 其 生 生 之 厚。

gài wén shàn shè shēng zhě
盖 闻 善 摄 生 者，

lù xíng bù yù sì hǔ
陆 行 不 遇 兕 虎，

rù jūn bù bèi jiǎ bīng
入 军 不 被 甲 兵。

sì wú suǒ tóu qí jiǎo
兕 无 所 投 其 角，

hǔ wú suǒ yòng qí zhǎo
虎 无 所 用 其 爪，

bīng wú suǒ róng qí rèn
兵 无 所 容 其 刃。

fū hé gù
夫 何 故？

yǐ qí wú sǐ dì
以 其 无 死 地。

The Great Gods of Three Realms, also named the Great Gods of the Three Elements. They rank only next to Jade Emperor in Daoist pantheon. They originated from nature worship of the sky, earth and water in early times. It was deemed that everything in the universe could not live without these three basic elements, which the Three Gods personify. People pray to the Three Element Gods for protection. It is believed that the Heaven Element God bestows happiness; the Earth Element God warns against crimes; the Water Element God exorcises bad spirits. The three gods take processions to exercise their duties. In this picture, they are structured in to three horizontal bands, and take different transportation tools according to their responsibilities, dragon in water, Kylin on earth, and flying chariot by air. They are all escorted by vast troops and many flags, presenting in an impressive manner.

三官乃道教中所奉之天官、地官、水官，亦称三元，地位仅次于玉皇大帝。天官赐福，地官赦罪，水官解厄，三官出巡旨在司察善恶，保护众生。画中三官各乘云驾水，旌幢扈从，威仪十足。布局三官分画，分成三层，并以云水区隔，这与大壁画的画法相同。

The Procession of the Great Gods of Three Realms, by Ma Lin, Song dynasty

三官出巡图　马麟　宋代

Chapter LI

Everything grows in accordance with
the divine law;
it is bred in its internal virtue,
formed by its environment,
and completed by external influence.
That is why all things
obey the divine law
and value their own virtue.
The divine law is omnimpotent
and virtue is valuable.
None orders them to obey,

dì wǔ shí yī zhāng
第 五 十 一 章

dào shēng zhī
道 生 之,

dé xù zhī
德 蓄 之,

wù xíng zhī
物 形 之,

shì chéng zhī
势 成 之。

shì yǐ wàn wù
是 以 万 物

mò bù zūn dào
莫 不 尊 道

ér guì dé
而 贵 德。

dào zhī zūn
道 之 尊,

dé zhī guì
德 之 贵,

fū mò zhī mìng
夫 莫 之 命

Long Wang or King of the Dragons in Daoism is the ruler of waters. Chinese dragons are traditionally regarded as water creatures. There are traditionally four principal Long Wangs, each governing one of the four oceans of the world. The four brothers Ao Kuang, Ao Run, Ao Shun, and Ao Qin serve the second highest deity in Chinese religion, the Jade Emperor. Each lives in a crystal palace and together they rule over armies of aquatic creatures who police the ocean depths. In addition to these four Long Wangs, local minor ones also exist, which numbers 185; they protect wells and rivers, and have particular power over rain. The local Long Wangs have large cults, and offerings are made to them in times of drought. When rain comes, a theatrical performance is held in honor of the Long Wangs. The depicted here is the Dragon King and his four sons. The female is Mrs. Anji, whose other name is Mazu or Heavenly Mother, and whose function is also strongly linked to the sea.

道经称：东南西北四海，皆有龙王总领其类，其下尚有一百八十五小龙王，具有兴云布雨的神力。四海龙王分别为东海龙王敖广、南海龙王敖润、西海龙王敖钦、北海龙王敖顺。图中女像为安济夫人。

Dragon Kings of the Four Seas, by an unknown author, Qing dynasty

四海龙王　清代

117

but they obey naturally.

In accordnce with the divine law

all things are bron and bred in

their virtue,

grown up and developped,

completed and matured,

protected and sheltered.

Creation without possession,

action without interference,

leadership without domination,

Such is the mysterious virtue.

ér cháng zì ráng
而 常 自 然。

gù dào shēng zhī
故 道 生 之。

dé xù zhī
德 蓄 之,

zhǎng zhī yù zhī
长 之 育 之,

chéng zhī shú zhī
成 之 熟 之,

gài zhī fù zhī
盖 之 覆 之。

shēng ér bù yǒu
生 而 不 有,

wèi ér bù shì
为 而 不 恃,

zhǎng ér bù zǎi
长 而 不 宰,

shì wèi xuán dé
是 谓 玄 德。

They are the guardians of heaven and Daoist altars. They implement holy orders and enhance the exorcising power of Daoist liturgies. The depicted are the thirty-six divine generals and other gods who are altogether making pilgrimage to the Jade Emperor.

道教有三十六员天将元帅神，他们护卫着天庭和道教的坛场，具有驱邪降魔、护正攘厄的威力，并能佐助行持。图中描绘的是部分三十六员天将神和其他神尊。

The Thirty-six Divine Generals Making Pilgrimage, by an unknown author

三十六员天将神朝圣图　无款

Chapter LII

The world has a beginning

regarded as its mother.

If you know the mother,

you can know her sons.

If you know her sons

and still follow the mother,

you may avoid danger all your life

long.

Dull your senses

and shut their doors,

you need not toil all your life.

Awake your senses

and satisfy them,

you will be incurable all your life.

Keen sight can see the smallest thing;

supple mind can resist the strongest

force.

Make use of light

to restore keen sight

without endangering yourself.

Let this be your habitual practice.

dì wǔ shí èr zhāng
第 五 十 二 章

tiān xià yǒu shǐ
天 下 有 始,

yǐ wéi tiān xià mǔ
以 为 天 下 母。

jì dé qí mǔ
既 得 其 母,

yǐ zhī qí zǐ
以 知 其 子。

jì zhī qí zǐ
既 知 其 子,

fù shǒu qí mǔ
复 守 其 母,

mò shēn bù dài
没 身 不 殆。

sè qí duì
塞 其 兑,

bì qí mén
闭 其 门,

zhōng shēn bù qín
终 身 不 勤。

kāi qí duì
开 其 兑,

jì qí shì
济 其 事,

zhōng shēn bù jiù
终 身 不 救。

jiàn xiǎo yuē míng
见 小 曰 明,

shǒu róu yuē qiáng
守 柔 曰 强。

yòng qí guāng
用 其 光,

fù guī qí míng
复 归 其 明。

wú yí shēn yāng
无 遗 身 殃,

shì wèi xí cháng
是 为 习 常。

The two immortal ladies are both dressed in clothes made of leafs and barks. The goat chariot is made of rattan and hay. The one who is picking up flowers seems to be younger and perhaps a attendant or disciple, the one who is standing with a cane behind the rock should be the master. The crane following closely to the master suggests that it can understand its master well. The far view of river addresses the transcendence from the mundane world. It is really a excellent vision of the primitive wonderland.

藤萝峭壁间，一女仙持仗，一鹤相随。一侍女以树叶为衣裳，双手攀花欲折。坡下方停着一辆羊车，结藤为输，颇为雅致。

The Immortals Domesticating a Crane and Picking up Flowers, by an unknown author, Song dynasty

画调鹤采花仙　宋代

Chapter LIII

Little as I know,

I will follow the great way,

only afraid to go astray.

The great way is even,

but people may like the by-path.

If the court is corrupt,

the fields waste,

and grenaries empty,

if lords are magnificently dressed,

carrying precious swords,

satiated with food and drink,

and poossessed of fabulous wealth,

they may be called thieves and robbers

not going the right way.

dì wǔ shí sān zhāng
第 五 十 三 章

shǐ wǒ jiè rán yǒu zhī
使 我 介 然 有 知，

xíng yú dà dào
行 于 大 道，

wéi shī shì wèi
惟 施 是 畏。

dà dào shèn yí
大 道 甚 夷，

ér mín hào jìng
而 民 好 径。

cháo shèn chú
朝 甚 除，

tián shèn wú
田 甚 芜，

cāng shèn xū
仓 甚 虚。

fú wén cǎi
服 文 采，

dài lì jiàn
带 利 剑，

yàn yǐn shí
厌 饮 食。

cái huò yǒu yú
财 货 有 余，

shì wèi dào yù
是 谓 盗 芋。

fēi dào yě zāi
非 道 也 哉。

Huang Daxian, literally translates to the Great Immortal Huang. He was born Huang Chu Ping in the middle fourth century in today's Lanxi City, Jinhua County , Zhejiang Province. He started practicing Daoism at fifteen when he encountered a Daoist master. After forty years of cultivation in a cave, he was elevated to the level of immortal and was able to transform stones into sheep. He is also known as Immortal Chisong, named after his hermit mountain. One of the most famous temple dedicated to him is Wong Tai Sin Temple in Hong Kong.

相传晋代道士黄初平被称为黄大仙，浙江省金华人，年幼家贫，替人牧羊，15 岁时在金华赤松山遇仙人，引至金华山石室中修道而成仙。他擅长法术，曾"叱石成羊"。本幅所画即此故事。又传说黄大仙也是赤松子。金华山曾在晋代建有赤松观，为江南道观之冠，信仰地区遍及中国东南，至华侨出外谋生，黄大仙信仰也随之传播。现今香港黄大仙庙，终年香火鼎盛，朝拜不绝，最为著名。

Transformation Miracle by Liu Songnian, Song dynasty

金华叱石　刘松年　宋代

Chapter LIV

What is well established cannot be rooted
up;

what is tightly held cannot slip away;

what is worshipped by descendants will

continue.

Cultivated in the person,

the virtue is true.

Cultivated in the family,

it is plentiful.

Cultivated in the country,

it is durable.

Cultivaled in the state.

it is abundant.

Cultivated in the world,

it is universal.

So judge another man by yourself,

another family by your family,

another country by your country,

another state by your state,

and the world by your world.

How can I know about the world?

Just in this way.

第五十四章

善建者不拔，

善抱者不脱。

子孙以祭祀不辍。

修之于身，

其德乃真；

修之于家，

其德乃余；

修之于乡，

其德乃长；

修之于国，

其德乃丰；

修之于天下，

其德乃普。

故以身观身，

以家观家，

以乡观乡，

以国观国，

以天下观天下。

吾何以知天下然哉？

以此。

北海真人知為誰坐
䭾靈龜食琀蛻虺
名御氣湲真誅風
雨雷電相追隨謹
息一閱九千歲凌空
遊行襤帶醉有
時光景照庭窓晉
得仰瞻清萬非
長洲沈周賀

The depicted character is a minor immortal in Daoism. He sits on the back of a turtle, roams on the water, with a carefree expression. The subtitle of the picture was written by Shen Zhou, a well known painter of Ming dynasty.

北海真人：道教中的一位神仙。这幅画北海真人，坐跨于灵龟之上，在水上遨游，神情洒脱自然。画上有明代著名画家沈周的题跋。

The Perfected Man of the North Sea, by Wu Wei, Ming dynasty

北海真人像　吴伟　明代

125

Chapter LV

A man of high virtue

may be compared to a new-born baby.

Poisonous insects do not sting their young,

nor do fierce beasts bite theirs.

The young have weak bones and supple muscles,

but their grasp is firm.

They know nothing about sex,

but their organ can be stirred,

for they have instinct.

They cry all day without becoming hoarse,

for their cry conforms to nature.

Knowing nature, one will be constant in action.

constant in action, one will be wise.

A body full of life is good；

a mind full of vigor is strong.

Anything past its prime will decline.

If you think it not in the right way,

you would be wrong.

dì wǔ shí wǔ zhāng
第 五 十 五 章

hán dé zhī hòu
含 德 之 厚，

bǐ yú chì zǐ
比 于 赤 子。

dú chóng bù shì
毒 虫 不 螫，

měng shòu bù jù
猛 兽 不 据，

jué niǎo bù bó
攫 鸟 不 搏。

gǔ ruò jīn róu ér wò gù
骨 弱 筋 柔 而 握 固，

wèi zhī pìn mǔ zhī hé ér suō zuò
未 知 牝 牡 之 合 而 朘 作，

jīng zhī zhì yě
精 之 至 也。

zhōng rì hào ér bù shà
终 日 号 而 不 嗄，

hé zhī zhì yě
和 之 至 也。

zhī hé yuē cháng
知 和 曰 常，

zhī cháng yuē míng
知 常 曰 明。

yì shēng yuē xiáng
益 生 曰 祥，

xīn shǐ qì yuē qiáng
心 使 气 曰 强。

wù zhuàng zé lǎo
物 壮 则 老，

wèi zhī bù dào
谓 之 不 道，

bù dào zǎo yǐ
不 道 早 已。

Yaochi means "Jade Moat", it is a special name for the heavenly palace of Queen Mother of the West. According to the mythical stories about Emperor Wu of Han dynasty, Queen Mother of the West once arrived at the emperor's palace, met him, and granted divine peaches to him. Since then the emperor often missed the scene. In this illustration, the terrace is surrounded by high mountains, pines are hanging over down from the cliffs, and clear streams are hitting the rocks. The Queen Mother and Emperor Wu are sitting on the jade terrace. The flags sets off along the mountain paths. Many immortals comes together to offer peaches as birthday gifts.

《汉武帝内传》称西王母驾临汉宫，与汉武帝相会，并送仙桃四枚。汉武帝常常思念此景。画中云峰匝饶，苍茸悬壁，清泉激岩。西王母上坐瑶台，山径中旗幡掩映，群仙毕至，皆捧仙桃祝寿。

Birthday Celebration in Yaochi, by Liu Songnian, Song dynasty

瑶池献寿图　刘松年　宋代

127

道德經
与
神仙画

Chapter LVI

Those who know do not speak；

those who speak do not know.

Dull your senses

and shut your door；

blunt the sharp

and solve the dispute；

soften the light

and mingle with dust

so as to be one with the mysterious law.

Therefore, none could be your friend

or your foe；

none could do you good

or harm；

none could honor you

or debase you.

So you are honored by the world.

dì wǔ shí wǔ zhāng
第 五 十 六 章

zhī zhě bù yán
知 者 不 言,

yán zhě bù zhī
言 者 不 知。

sè qí duì
塞 其 兑,

bì qí mén
闭 其 门;

cuò qí ruì
挫 其 锐,

jiě qí fēn
解 其 纷;

hé qí guāng
和 其 光,

tōng qí chén
同 其 尘;

shì wèi xuán tóng
是 谓 玄 同。

gù bù kě dé ér qīn
故 不 可 得 而 亲,

bù kě dé ér shū
不 可 得 而 疏;

bù kě dé ér lì
不 可 得 而 利,

bù kě dé ér hài
不 可 得 而 害;

bù kě dé ér guì
不 可 得 而 贵,

bù kě dé ér jiàn
不 可 得 而 贱。

gù wéi tiān xià guì
故 为 天 下 贵。

The three brothers are Maoying, Maogu and Mao'ai, who are the founders of Maoshan Sect. Maoshan or Mount Mao lying across the four counties of Jurong, Jintan, Lishui, and Liyang in Jiangsu Province, is named after the three Maos, and therefore is also the birthplace of the sect.

三茅真君即茅盈、茅固、茅衷兄弟三
人，是道教茅山派的祖师。相传茅盈18
岁弃家修道，先后遇西城王君、西王母
授以道要，入居茅山修真道成。后其弟
茅固、茅衷皆弃官随兄学道，兄弟三人
一起成仙。

Mao Brothers, by an unknown author, Ming dynasty

三茅真君　明代

Chapter LVII

Rule the state in an ordinary way,

but fight the war in an extraodinary way.

Win the world by doing nothing wrong.

How can I know this is right?

For the following reasons:

More prohibitions in the world

will impoverish people;

more armed people

will bring more trouble to the state;

more cunning people

will do more shrewd tricks;

more laws and decrees

will make more outlaws.

dì wǔ shí qī zhāng
第 五 十 七 章

yǐ zhèng zhì guó
以 正 治 国,

yǐ qí yòng bīng
以 奇 用 兵,

yǐ wú shì qǔ tiān xià
以 无 事 取 天 下。

wú hé yǐ zhī qí rán zāi
吾 何 以 知 其 然 哉?

yǐ cǐ
以 此:

tiān xià duō jì huì
天 下 多 忌 讳

ér mín mí pín
而 民 弥 贫;

mín duō lì qì
民 多 利 器,

guó jiā zī hūn
国 家 滋 昏。

rén duō jì qiǎo
人 多 伎 巧

qí wù zī qǐ
奇 物 滋 起。

fǎ lìng zī zhāng
法 令 滋 彰,

dào zéi duō yǒu
盗 贼 多 有。

The Emperor of Fengdu is the head official of the nether world. It is reported that Wang Fangping and Ying Changsheng of Han dynasty once cultivated in Fengdu County, Sichuan Province before they ascended to heaven. Later, these two immortals amalgamated into the King of the Nether World and Fengdu became "the city of ghosts".

酆都大帝又称"北阴大帝君"，为阴间诸鬼之总管。传说汉代仙人王方平、阴长生曾在四川酆都县酆都山得道升仙，二人合成"阴王"，后传为阴间神王，酆都成为"鬼城"，此地遂成酆都大帝之治所。

The Emperor of Fengdu, by an unknown author

酆都大帝

Therefors, the sage says:

If I do nothing wrong,

the people will go the right way；

if I love peace,

the people will not go to war；

if I do not impoverish them,

they will become rich；

if I have no selfish desire,

they will naturally be simple.

gù shèng rén yún
故 圣 人 云：

wǒ wú wéi
我 无 为

ér mín zì huà
而 民 自 化。

wǒ hào jìng
我 好 静

ér mín zì zhèng
而 民 自 正。

wǒ wú shì
我 无 事

ér mín zì fù
而 民 自 富。

wǒ wú yù
我 无 欲

ér mín zì pǔ
而 民 自 朴。

This picture is about the story of Perfected Master Xu's family and their pets transferring to the wonderland. Perfected Master Xu, whose first name is Jingzhi, was born in Runan County, Jin dynasty(265~420). He once was the local governor of Jingyang County before he secluded from the war. Xu and his family, together with their pets ascended to paradise in Ningkang era(373~376).

此画描绘着许真人骑牛，携带家眷牲口，迁往仙境情景，许真人名逊，字敬之，晋朝汝南人。曾当过旌阳令，后来因世乱而归隐。宁康初年在洪州西山，许真人与家人连同鸡犬，一齐飞升而去。

The Journey to Wonderland together with Pets, by Cui Zizhong, Ming dynasty

云中鸡犬　崔子忠　明代

Chapter LVIII

If the government is lenient,

the people will be simple.

If the government is severe,

the people will feel a lack of freedom.

Weal comes after wos;

woe lies under weal.

Who knows the line of demarcation?

There is no absolute norm.

The normal may turn into the abnormal;

the good may turn into evil.

The peolpe are perplexed

for a long, long time.

Therefore the sage is fair and square

without a cutting edge,

thrifty but not exacting,

straightforward but not haughty,

bright but not dazzling.

dì wǔ shí bā zhāng
第 五 十 八 章

qí zhèng mèn mèn
其 政 闷 闷,

qí mín chún chún
其 民 淳 淳;

qí zhèng chá chá
其 政 察 察,

qí mín quē quē
其 民 缺 缺。

huò xī fú zhī suǒ yǐ
祸 兮 福 之 所 倚,

fú xī huò zhī suǒ fú
福 兮 祸 之 所 伏。

shú zhī qí jí
孰 知 其 极?

qí wú zhèng
其 无 正。

zhèng fù wéi qí
正 复 为 奇,

shàn fù wéi yāo
善 复 为 妖。

rén zhī mí
人 之 迷,

qí rì gù jiǔ
其 日 固 久。

shì yǐ shèng rén
是 以 圣 人

fāng ér bù gē
方 而 不 割,

lián ér bù guì
廉 而 不 刿,

zhí ér bù sì
直 而 不 肆,

guāng ér bù yào
光 而 不 耀。

Lü Dongbin Demonstrating on Yueyang Tower, by an unknown author, Southern Song dynasty

吕洞宾显圣岳阳楼　南宋

Yueyang Tower, built in Tang dynasty, is the most important attraction of Yueyang City and listed among the three most famous ancient towers in south China. It is reported that he has removed the mythical flood dragons in the area between Yangtse River and Huai River, played with crane and got drunken three times on Yueyang Tower. This picture is about the episode of frenzy excitement when people recognized the immortal's identity.

岳阳楼是洞庭湖畔的著名建筑，江南三大名楼之一，始建于唐代，传说吕洞宾曾在江淮一带斩杀蛟龙，岳阳戏鹤并三醉岳阳楼等故事。此图所绘吕洞宾飘然虚空，楼上人们作揖观望的盛况。

Chapter LIX

To rule people and serve heaven,

nothing is better than frugality.

Only by frugality

can one conform early to the divine law.

Early conformity means accumulation

of virtue；

with virtue accmulated,

there is no difficulty but can be

overcome；

with difficulty overcome,

one's power knows no limit.

With unlimited power one can rule the

state；

a state called one's motherland can long,

long last,

for the sturdy stalk is deep-rooted.

Such is the way of everlasting existence.

dì wǔ shí jiǔ zhāng
第 五 十 九 章

zhì rén shì tiān
治 人 事 天,

mò ruò sè
莫 若 啬。

fú wéi sè
夫 唯 啬,

shì wèi zǎo fú
是 谓 早 服。

zǎo fú　wèi zhi zhōng ji dé
早 服, 谓 之 重 积 德;

zhōng ji dé　zé wú bù kè
重 积 德, 则 无 不 克;

wú bù kè　zé mò zhi qí ji
无 不 克, 则 莫 知 其 极;

mò zhi qí ji　kě yǐ yǒu guó
莫 知 其 极, 可 以 有 国;

yǒu guó zhi mǔ　kě yǐ cháng jiǔ
有 国 之 母, 可 以 长 久。

shì wèi shēn gēn gù dǐ
是 谓 深 根 固 柢,

chángshēng jiǔ shì zhi dào
长 生 久 视 之 道。

The three immortals making elixir are Immortal Lady He, Iron-crutch Li and Elder Zhang Guo (Zhang Guo Lao). The smoke curls upwards, obscures some parts of the picture, and impresses people with a mysterious spectacle.

炼丹图绘何仙姑、铁拐李与张果老三仙围炉炼丹，炉烟袅袅，虚实相映间，倍觉气势逼人。

The Elixir Making, by Huang Shen, Qing dynasty

炼丹图　黄慎　清代

Chapter LX

A large state should be ruled as a small fish is cooked.

If the world is ruled in conformity with the divine law,

the spirits will lose their supernatural power.

Not that they have lost their power,

but that their power will do no harm.

Not only will their power do no harm,

but the sage will not harm them either.

Since neither will harm the other,

so virtue belongs to both.

dì liù shí zhāng
第 六 十 章

zhì dà guó
治 大 国，

ruò pēng xiǎo xiān
若 烹 小 鲜。

yǐ dào lì tiān xià
以 道 莅 天 下，

qí guǐ bù shén
其 鬼 不 神；

fēi qí guǐ bù shén
非 其 鬼 不 神，

qí shén bù shāng rén
其 神 不 伤 人；

fēi qí shén bù shāng rén
非 其 神 不 伤 人，

shèng rén yì bù shāng rén
圣 人 亦 不 伤 人。

fū liǎng bù xiāng shāng
夫 两 不 相 伤，

gù dé jiāo guī yān
故 德 交 归 焉。

The three constellations are the escorts or the Big Dipper. In Daoism, it is believed that the North Pole constellations can control the life and success of people, so they are worshipped for longevity.

三台星君，即上台、中台和下台。又称"三阶"、"三衡""三奇"等名。上台虚精开德星君，中台六淳司空星君，下台曲生司禄星君。乃宿星之尊，和阴阳而理万物也。

The Constellations of Three Terraces, by an unknown author

三台星君　无款　清代

139

Chapter LXI

A large state lies downstream in a low
position,

where run all the steams.

In the intercourse of the world,

the female and win the male

by lying still in a lower position.

So if a large state takes a lower position,

it may win over a small state.

If a small atate takes a lower position,

it may win a large state.

So a lower position may win

or win over another state.

A large state will only rule and peotect,

and a small state will be ruled and

protected.

Both states may attain their end,

so a large state had better take a lower

position.

dì liù shí yi zhāng
第 六 十 一 章

dà guó zhě xià liú
大 国 者 下 流,

tiān xià zhī jiāo
天 下 之 交。

tiān xià zhī jiāo
天 下 之 交,

pìn cháng yǐ jìng shèng mǔ
牝 常 以 静 胜 牡,

yǐ jìng wéi xià
以 静 为 下。

gù dà guó yǐ xià xiǎo guó
故 大 国 以 下 小 国,

zé qǔ xiǎo guó
则 取 小 国。

xiǎo guó yǐ xià dà guó
小 国 以 下 大 国,

zé qǔ dà guó
则 取 大 国。

gù huò xià yǐ qǔ
故 或 下 以 取,

huò xià ér qǔ
或 下 而 取。

dà guó bù guò yù jiān xù rén
大 国 不 过 欲 兼 畜 人。

xiǎo guó bù guò yù rù shì rén
小 国 不 过 欲 入 事 人。

fū liǎng zhě gè dé suǒ yù
夫 两 者 各 得 所 欲,

dà zhě yí wéi xià
大 者 宜 为 下。

The freaky rocks, old pines, gnarled cane, the bowl made from a burl and the two immortal ladies in idiosyncratic dressings compose a age-old picture.

此幅作磐石寿松，仙姑二人。奇松
异石，人物造型特色分明，有奇古
之气。

The Immortal Ladies Celebrating Birthday, by Chen Hongshou, Ming dynasty

仙人献寿　陈洪绶　明代

Chapter LXII

The divine law is the key to everything:

the treasure for men of virtue,

the protection for men without virtue.

Fair words can win respect

and fair deeds can influence people.

Even though without virtue,

why should they be abandoned?

Therefors the emperor is enthroned

and the three ministers installed.

Though a chariot of four steeds

precceded by jadewares may be

presented,

it is not so good as to proclaim the law

divine.

Why should the ancients

value the divine law?

Is it not said that who seeks will find

and who sins will be pardoned?

That is why the divine law is valued in

the world.

dì liù shí ér zhāng
第 六 十 二 章

dào zhě
道 者，

wàn wù zhī ào
万 物 之 奥。

shàn rén zhī bǎo
善 人 之 宝，

bù shàn rén zhī suǒ bǎo
不 善 人 之 所 保。

měi yán kě yǐ shì zūn
美 言 可 以 市 尊，

měi xíng kě yǐ jiā rén
美 行 可 以 加 人。

rén zhī bù shàn
人 之 不 善，

hé qì zhī yǒu
何 弃 之 有？

gù lì tiān zǐ
故 立 天 子，

zhì sān gōng
置 三 公。

suī yǒu gǒng bì
虽 有 拱 璧

yǐ xiān sì mǎ
以 先 驷 马，

bù rú zuò jìn cǐ dào
不 如 坐 进 此 道。

gù zhī suǒ yǐ
古 之 所 以

guì cǐ dào zhě hé
贵 此 道 者 何？

bù yuē qiú zhī yǐ dé
不 曰 求 之 以 得，

yǒu zuì yǐ miǎn xié
有 罪 以 免 邪？

gù wéi tiān xià guì
故 为 天 下 贵。

Founder Master Lü Crossing the Dongting Lake, by an unknown author

吕祖过洞庭图

What is amazing is the restful and calm expression of Master Lü on the voyage of waves.

"洞庭"及洞庭湖。图绘吕祖穿白衣飘然水上，一派仙风道骨的气概。

Chapter LXIII

Do nothing wrong!

do a deed as if it were not a deed;

take the tasteful as if it were tasteless.

Big or small, more or less,

any difficulty has an easy part,

any great deed has a small detail.

There is nothing difficult

but consists of easy parts;

there is no great deed

but consists of small details.

Therefore the sage

never tries to be great,

but at last he becomes great.

A rash promise will soon be broken;

much underestimation will entail much

difficulty.

Therefore the sage antecipates all

difficulties,

so there is nothing difficult in the end.

dì liù shí sān zhāng
第 六 十 三 章

wéi wú wéi
为 无 为,

shì wú shì
事 无 事,

wèi wú wèi
味 无 味。

dà xiǎo duǒ shǎo
大 小 多 少,

bào yuàn yǐ dé
报 怨 以 德。

tú nán yú qí yì
图 难 于 其 易,

wèi dà yú qí xì
为 大 于 其 细。

tiān xià nán shì
天 下 难 事

bì zuò yú yì
必 作 于 易。

tiān xià dà shì
天 下 大 事

bì zuò yú xì
必 作 于 细。

shì yǐ shèng rén
是 以 圣 人

zhōng bù wéi dà
终 不 为 大,

gù néng chéng qí dà
故 能 成 其 大。

fū qīng nuò bì guǎ xìn
夫 轻 诺 必 寡 信。

duō yì bì duō nán
多 易 必 多 难。

shì yǐ shèng rén yóu nán zhī
是 以 圣 人 犹 难 之,

gù zhōng wú nán yǐ
故 终 无 难 矣。

The three hermits are sitting round some food and drink under the weeping willows by a riverbank, and listening attentively to some attractive sounds, which must be the singing of some warblers. The three attendants seem enjoying the natural music very much too. The river flows slowly, giving out the aroma of a warm spring.

三位高士围坐岸边垂柳下，酒肴杯盘放置其间，三位侍者连同主人都在侧耳倾听，点出鹂鸟正在鸣叫，动人心弦。背景一水横亘，似乎可感到愠愠的春气。

Listening to the Warblers with a Bowl of Liquor, by Zhang Chong , Ming dynasty

斗酒听鹂图　张翀　明代

Chapter LXIV

It is easy to hold what is stable,

to plan before troubles should rise,

to break what is fragile,

to disperse what is small.

Make preparations before things

happen；

keep order before disorder sets in.

A huge tree

grows out of a small shoot；

a nine-storied tower

rises from a heap of earth；

a thousand-mile journey

begin with the firth step.

Who is too eager for success will fail,

dì liù shí sì zhāng
第 六 十 四 章

qí ān yì chí
其 安 易 持，

qí wèi zhào yì móu
其 未 兆 易 谋，

qí cuì yì pàn
其 脆 易 泮，

qí wēi yì sàn
其 微 易 散。

wèi zhī yú wèi yǒu
为 之 于 未 有，

zhì zhī yú wèi luàn
治 之 于 未 乱。

hé bào zhī mù
合 抱 之 木

shēng yú háo mò
生 于 毫 末。

jiǔ céng zhī tái
九 层 之 台

qǐ yú lèi tǔ
起 于 累 土。

qiān lǐ zhī xíng
千 里 之 行

shǐ yú zú xià
始 于 足 下。

wèi zhě bài zhī
为 者 败 之，

Guan Yu and his Captive, by Shang Xi, Ming dynasty

关羽擒将图　商喜　明代

Guan Yu (160-219) was a military general under the warlord Liu Bei during the late Eastern Han Dynasty and Three Kingdoms period. While his life stories have largely given way to semi-fictional ones throughout East Asia, in which his deeds and moral qualities have been much exaggerated. He has been deified and worshipped as "Holy Emperor Guan" or "Guandi", the god of war and wealth, and been seen as the epitome of loyalty and righteousness. Guandi is traditionally portrayed as a red-faced warrior with a long lush beard, but this picture misses his weapon guandao which resembles a halberd and weighs 82 jin (41 kilograms using today's standards). The two generals standing beside him is Guan Ping and Zhou Chang.

画面中三国名将关羽赤面凤眼，长髯伟躯倚石而坐，两旁周仓，关平侍立。关公，又称"关圣帝君"，简称"关帝"，有"驱邪避恶，诛罚叛逆，司命禄，庇护商贾，招财进宝"之作用，因其忠义，又被奉为财神。

147

道德經与神仙画

too eager forgain will lose.

Therefore, the sage does nothing for success

so he will not fail;

he holds nothing too tight to lose.

People engaged in a task

often fail on the brink of success.

If cautious from the beginning to the end,

they would not have failed.

Therefore, the sage desires to be desireless;

he never values what is hard to get;

he learns to be unlearned.

He tries to mend the fault of others,

and to help all things develop naturally

without his interference.

zhí zhě shī zhī
执 者 失 之。

shì yǐ shèng rén wú wéi
是 以 圣 人 无 为

gù wú bài
故 无 败,

wú zhí gù wú shī
无 执 故 无 失。

mín zhī cóng shì
民 之 从 事

cháng yú jǐ chéng ér bài zhī
常 于 几 成 而 败 之。

shèn zhōng rú shǐ
慎 终 如 始,

zé wú bài shì
则 无 败 事。

shì yǐ shèng rén yù bù yù
是 以 圣 人 欲 不 欲,

bù guì nán dé zhī huò
不 贵 难 得 之 货,

xué bù xué
学 不 学。

fù zhòng rén zhī suǒ guò
复 众 人 之 所 过,

yǐ fǔ wàn wù zhī zì rán
以 辅 万 物 之 自 然,

ér bù gǎn wéi
而 不 敢 为。

The Craggy Mount Huang, by Shi Tao, Qing dynasty

黄山奇峰　石涛　清代

Mount Huang under the brush of the grand artist is like a wonderland. The peaks gleaming in the mist, the old pines stretching friendly and the hermits playing on the terrace, all are the parts of a different world.

黄山云海中，若隐若现的山峰，在画家笔下早已变成另外一个神仙世界，山上有仙人玩耍，奇松舒展，云气淋漓。

Chapter LXV

The ancients who followed the divine law

would not enlighten the public mind

but simplify it.

The people would be unruly

because they are sophisticated.

To rule the state sophistically

is to do harm to it;

to rule it unsophistically

is to do it good.

There are two models of sophistication.

The knowledge of models

is called mysterious virtue.

The mysterious virtue is profound and far-reaching.

it returns to nature with all things,

and becomes perfectly natural in the end.

dì liù shí wǔ zhāng
第 六 十 五 章

gǔ zhī shàn wèi dào zhě
古 之 善 为 道 者，

fēi yǐ míng mín
非 以 明 民，

jiāng yǐ yú zhī
将 以 愚 之。

mín zhī nán zhì
民 之 难 治，

yǐ qí zhì duō
以 其 智 多。

gù yǐ zhì zhì guó guó zhī zéi
故 以 智 治 国，国 之 贼。

bù yǐ zhì zhì guó guó zhī fú
不 以 智 治 国，国 之 福。

zhī cǐ liǎng zhě
知 此 两 者，

yì jī shì
亦 稽 式。

cháng zhī jī shì
常 知 稽 式，

shì wèi xuán dé
是 谓 玄 德。

xuán dé shēn yǐ yuǎn yǐ
玄 德 深 矣，远 矣！

yú wù fǎn yǐ
与 物 反 矣，

rán hòu nǎi zhì dà shùn
然 后 乃 至 大 顺。

Huanghe Lou or Yellow Crane Tower is in Wuhan by Yangtze River, Hubei province. It is said that there was an immortal neophyte once passed over this place by ridding a yellow crane, therefore it is named this way. Another tale is about that Fei Wenwei of Sichuan stopped here on his way of ascending to heaven by a yellow crane. This building was reported having been constructed in the second year of Huangwu era of Wu state (223 CE). After that it has been destroyed and rebuilt for many times. There are many inscriptions by famous poets. This picture is about the story of the immortal, crane and the tower.

黄鹤楼故址在湖北省武汉市蛇山黄鹤湾，临长江。古代传说，有仙人子安，乘黄鹤过此，故名。一说，蜀费文炜登仙，曾驾黄鹤憩此。相传始建于吴黄武二年，历代屡毁屡建，诗人题咏亦多。画幅右侧中间，有仙人乘鹤飞去，楼台间，众人仰头目视，这幅画即是写此故事。

The Yellow Crane Tower, by an unknown author, Song dynasty

黄鹤楼图　宋代

Chapter LXVI

The sea can lord it

over all the streams flowing from the

vales,

for it takes a lower position,

so water flows into it from hundreds of

vales.

If you want to be higher than the people,

you must learn to be humble in words；

if you wang to go before them,

you must learn to stay behind in person.

So when the sage is high above,

the people do not feel his weight；

when he is at their head,

they feel no harm.

That is why the world praises him

without getting tired.

As he will not contend,

so none in the world can contend with

him.

dì liù shí liù zhāng
第 六 十 六 章

jiāng hǎi zhī suǒ yǐ néng
江 海 之 所 以 能

wèi bǎi gǔ wáng zhě
为 百 谷 王 者，

yǐ qí shàn xià zhī
以 其 善 下 之，

gù néng wèi bǎi gǔ wāng
故 能 为 百 谷 王。

shì yǐ shèng rén yù shàng mín
是 以 圣 人 欲 上 民，

bì yǐ yán xià zhī
必 以 言 下 之。

yù xiān mín
欲 先 民，

bì yǐ shēn hòu zhī
必 以 身 后 之。

shì yǐ shèng rén chù shàng
是 以 圣 人 处 上，

ér mín bù zhòng
而 民 不 重；

chù qián
处 前，

ér mín bù hài
而 民 不 害。

shì yǐ tiān xià lè tuī
是 以 天 下 乐 推

ér bù yàn
而 不 厌。

yǐ qí bù zhēng
以 其 不 争，

gù tiān xià mò néng yǔ zhī zhēng
故 天 下 莫 能 与 之 争。

Exhortation from Skeleton, selected from the frescoes in Yongle Temple, Yuan dynasty

叹骷髅（永乐宫壁画局部）　元代

This is a story about Wang Chongyang, the founder master of Quanzhen (all true) Daoism. He is teaching the truth of impermanence with a picture of skeleton.

此图描绘王重阳在山东收徒传道，并以"骷髅图"警示弟子，传授道法。

王重阳—全真道的创始人，元世祖袭封为"重阳全真开化真君"，是道教历史上著名人物。

Chapter LXVII

All the world says my divine law is great,

and there is nothing like it.

Since it is great,

so nothing can be like it.

If there is anything like it,

it would not have been so great.

I have three treasures

which I hold and keep:

the first is magnanimity,

the second is frugality,

and the third is humility to be the last of

the world.

dì liù shí qī zhāng
第 六 十 七 章

tiān xià jiē wèi wǒ dào dà
天 下 皆 谓 我 道 大，

sì bù xiào
似 不 肖。

fū wéi dà
夫 唯 大，

gù sì bù xiào
故 似 不 肖。

ruò xiào
若 肖，

jiǔ yǐ qí xì yě fū
久 矣 其 细 也 夫。

wǒ yǒu sān bǎo
我 有 三 宝，

chí ér bǎo zhī
持 而 保 之：

yī yuē cí
一 曰 慈，

èr yuē jiǎn
二 曰 俭，

sān yuē bù gǎn wéi tiān xià xiān
三 曰 不 敢 为 天 下 先。

Liu Haichan once excelled in the imperial examination of the Later Liang dynasty (907-923) and served as the prime minister. Liu was fond of Huang-Lao doctrines. One day Zhongli Quan, one of the Eight Immortals , came to him and asked him for ten coins and ten eggs, piled them all one on another on the table. Haichan was frightened and cried, "It is dangerous! It is dangerous!" The Zhongli said, "No, no. There is less danger than your own life." Haichan grasped what he meant immediately. He resigned from the officialdom next morning and followed him to be a hermit in Mount Zhongnan, Shaanxi. Later he became a disciple of Lü Dongbin and cultivate alchemy. He is portrayed with a toad in hands and a string of coins on the waist bell, because his first name Haichan signifies Sea Toad, and his story of coins which means to be nonchalant to wealth and success.

此画刘海双目凝视，戏手中金蟾，腰间挂钱与葫芦。刘海乃道教南宗始祖，名操，本为辽代进士，因好黄老之学，弃官从正阳子隐居终南后成仙而去。元世祖时封为"明悟弘道真君"。刘海以洒钱意为放弃功名利禄、淡泊修行，中国民间传有"刘海戏金蟾、步步钓金钱"的说法，赞扬淡薄名利人之品格。

Liu Haichan, by an unknown author, Yuan dynasty

刘海像　元代

155

The magnaminous can be courgcous,

the frugal can be generous,

the humble last of the world

can become leader of the people.

For courage without magnanimity,

generosity without frugality

the front without the rear

are doomed to failure.

The magnanimous will be victorious in war

and steadfast in defence.

Heaven would favor them

and protect them with magnanimity.

cí gù néng yǒng
慈 故 能 勇，

jiǎn gù néng guǎng
俭 故 能 广，

bù gǎn wéi tiān xià xiān
不 敢 为 天 下 先，

gù néng chéng qì zhǎng
故 能 成 器 长。

jīn shě cí qiě yǒng
今 舍 慈 且 勇，

shě jiǎn qiě guǎng
舍 俭 且 广，

shě hòu qiě xiān
舍 后 且 先，

sǐ yǐ
死 矣！

fū cí
夫 慈，

yǐ zhàn zé shèng
以 战 则 胜，

yǐ shǒu zé gù
以 守 则 固。

tiān jiāng jiù zhī
天 将 救 之，

yǐ cí wèi zhī
以 慈 卫 之。

The Dream of a Butterfly, by an unknown author, Ming dynasty

梦蝶图　明代

One day Zhuangzi dozed off and dreamed that he turned into a butterfly. He flapped his wings and sure enough he was a butterfly, he completely forgot that he was Zhuangzi. Soon though, he realized that that proud butterfly was really Zhuangzi who dreamed he was a butterfly, or was it a butterfly who dreamed he was Zhuangzi!

此图描绘的是，战国时期著名的哲学家庄子，梦见自己化成了蝴蝶，翩翩而飞，竟然忘记了自己是庄子。醒来后不知道是自己化成了蝴蝶，还是蝴蝶化成了自己。

Chapter LXVIII

A good warrior is not violent,

a good fighter is not angry,

a good victor will not yield,

a good leader will be humble.

Such is the virtue of non-contention,

the ability of employing men.

Such is the way to match heaven.

dì liù shi bā zhāng
第 六 十 八 章

shàn wèi shì zhě bù wǔ
善 为 士 者 不 武,

shàn zhàn zhě bù nù
善 战 者 不 怒,

shàn shàng dí zhě bù yǔ
善 胜 敌 者 不 与,

shàn yòng rén zhě wèi zhī xià
善 用 人 者 为 之 下。

shì wèi bù zhēng zhī dé
是 谓 不 争 之 德,

shì wèi yòng rén zhī lì
是 谓 用 人 之 力,

shì wèi pèi tiān zhī jí
是 谓 配 天 之 极。

In Chinese his name is Xuanwu or Zhenwu, literally meaning "Dark General" or "Perfect General", because he is the God of the Northern Lunar Mansions, the Black God of the North among the Five Element Gods. According to Daoist scriptures, Zhenwu was originally a prince of the Pure Happy Kingdom, but he did not want to succeed to the throne. Instead he swore to kill all demons in the world, and went to Mount Taihe to cultivate Dao. After he had mastered Dao, he was sent by the Jade Emperor to guard the north. The Jade Emperor renamed Mount Taihe as Mount Wudang, which means "no one can undertake this post except Zhenwu". He usually takes the image of a man wearing long flowing hair with black armor and clothing, stepping on a turtle-snake statue with bare feet.

真武大帝原称"玄武大帝"，亦称"真武帝君"、道教徒俗称"无量祖师"。道书记载真武大帝原为净乐国太子，入太和山修道四十二载，功成德满，玉帝敕镇北方，为真武大帝。太和山因改名为武当山，意为非"真武不足以当之"。

Emperor Zhenwu, by an unknown author

真武大帝

Chapter LXIX

A strategist said:

"I will not take the offensive but the defensive;

I will not advance an inch and retreat a foot."

For this means marching without advancing,

raising arms without striking,

holding when there is no weapon,

and stiking when there is no enemy.

No danger is geater that making light of the foe,

which may lead to the loss of my treasure.

When two fighting forces are equal in strength,

the wronged side will win the victory.

dì liù shí jiǔ zhāng
第 六 十 九 章

yòng bīng yǒu yán
用 兵 有 言 :

wú bù gǎn wéi zhǔ ér wèi kè
吾 不 敢 为 主 而 为 客 ,

bù gǎn jìn cùn ér tuì chǐ
不 敢 进 寸 而 退 尺 。

shì wèi háng wú háng
是 谓 行 无 行 。

rǎng wú bì
攘 无 臂 。

zhí wú bīng
执 无 兵 ,

réng wú dí
扔 无 敌 。

huò mò dà yú qīng dí
祸 莫 大 于 轻 敌 ,

qīng dí jī sàng wú bǎo
轻 敌 几 丧 吾 宝 。

gù kàng bīng xiāng ruò
故 抗 兵 相 若 ,

āi zhě shèng yǐ
哀 者 胜 矣 。

He is one of the second most ancient of the
Eight Immortals. He is also known as Zhongli
of Han because he was born in the Han Dynasty.
Zhongli Quan was a general serving the Han
Dynasty. It is told that he enlightened Lü
Dongbin into immortal, He is usually depicted
with his chest and belly bare and holding a fan.
The fan has the magical ability of reviving the
dead.

钟离权：八仙之一，又称汉钟离。相传
钟离权曾度吕洞宾成道。其形象常是头
上扎髻，龙睛虬髯，坦腹自若，是历代
画师喜绘的题材。

Zhongli Quan, by Zhaolin, Ming dynasty
钟离权　赵麒　明代

Chapter LXX

It is very easy to understand what I say

and put it into practice.

But it is not understood

and not put into practice in the world.

My words show what I worship;

my deeds show whom I serve.

People do not know my words,

so they do not understand me,

Few people understand me,

so I am sll the more valuable.

That is why the sage wears plain clothes,

but his heart is pure as jade.

dì qī shí zhāng
第 七 十 章

wú yán shèn yì zhī
吾 言 甚 易 知，

shè yì xíng
甚 易 行。

tiān xià mò néng zhī
天 下 莫 能 知，

mò néng xíng
莫 能 行。

yán yǒu zōng
言 有 宗，

shì yǒu jūn
事 有 君。

fū wéi wú zhī
夫 唯 无 知，

shì yǐ wú wǒ zhī
是 以 无 我 知。

zhī wǒ zhě xī
知 我 者 希，

zé wǒ guì yǐ
则 我 贵 矣。

shì yǐ shèng rén pī hè ér huái yù
是 以 圣 人 被 褐 而 怀 玉。

Tang Di was a painter of the Yuan dynasty, who excelled in painting landscapes. He established a smooth and bold style of strokes and a graceful hues. In this picture, some fishermen (maybe hermits) are walking slowly and leisurely, and talking cheerfully and humorously on the pathway back on a frosty autumn dusk. The old trees on rugged land and the very long moss strips hanging from the curling branches, seem also telling about a lot of joys of being aloof from the mundane affairs.

奇石杂树高高耸立，松树虬曲的枝干上爬满了藤萝，秋色含霜，几名渔人逍遥的走在小路上，闲步笑语，缓缓而行。

On the Way Back from Fishing, by Tang Di, Yuan dynasty

霜蒲归渔图　唐棣　元代

163

Chapter LXXI

It is good to know that you do not know；

it is wrong to pretend to know what you

do not.

Since you know what is wrong,

so you will not be wrong.

The sage is not wrong,

for he knows what is wrong,

so he will do no wrong.

dì qī shí yī zhāng
第 七 十 一 章

zhī bù zhī shàng
知 不 知 上；

bù zhī zhī bìng
不 知 知 病。

fū wéi bìng bìng
夫 唯 病 病，

shì yǐ bù bìng
是 以 不 病。

shèng rén bù bìng
圣 人 不 病，

yǐ qí bìng bìng
以 其 病 病，

shì yǐ bù bìng
是 以 不 病。

Qin Gao is reported to have lived during the Warring States period (403-221 BCE). He was skilled at playing Chinese harp (qin) and was an imperial advisor. Qin Gao studied occult skill and mastered the secrets of immortality. Supposedly, he roamed in the Jizhou region, present-day Hebei, for more than 200 years until one day he rode a dragon into the waters. However, wishing to keep a promised meeting with a disciple, on the specified day Qin Gao emerged from the depths riding on a huge red carp. In painting Qin Gao is usually seen on the back of a fish, wearing a scholar's cap on his head.

此图绘古代琴高乘鲤的神话故事,《列仙传》载:琴高为战国时赵国人,善鼓琴曾为宋唐王舍人,有长生之术。后遁入涿水中取龙子,临行与诸弟子约期相见,嘱在河旁设祠堂及设斋等候他复出。届时,琴高,果然乘赤鲤从水中出,留一月余,又乘鲤入水。此图即琴高辞别弟子乘鲤而去之景。布局构思精巧,云雾弥漫,栩栩如生。

Qingao Riding on Carp, by Li Zai, Ming dynasty

琴高乘鲤图　李在　明代

165

Chapter LXXII

If the people fear no power,

it shows that their power is great.

Do not deprive them of their houses,

nor interfere in their life.

If you do not interfere in their affair,

they will not interfere in yours.

Therefore the sage know himself

but does not show off;

he respects but does not overalue

himself.

Thus he prefers that to this.

dì qi shí èr zhāng
第 七 十 二 章

mín bù wèi wēi
民 不 畏 威,

zé dà wēi zhì
则 大 威 至。

wú xiá qí suǒ jū
无 狎 其 所 居,

wú yàn qí suǒ shēng
无 厌 其 所 生。

fū wéi bù yàn
夫 唯 不 厌,

shì yǐ bù yàn
是 以 不 厌。

shì yǐ shèng rén
是 以 圣 人

zì zhī bù zì jiàn
自 知 不 自 见,

zì ài bù zì guì
自 爱 不 自 贵。

gù qù bǐ qǔ cǐ
故 去 彼 取 此。

Zhang Ziyang(984~1082), whose personal name was Boduan, and Ziyang is his style name. He was born in Tiantai, Zhejiang province in Northern Song dynasty. He started to study Daoism in his boyhood. After that, he became a successful candidate in the national civil service examination, but then was exiled to the southern border. In the second Xining year of the Northern Song dynasty(1069), his perseverance and devotion moved a certain Perfect man so much in Chengdu that he taught Zhang with Inner Alchemical secrets. After he published his work On Realizing Perfection, many people came to follow him. So he became the founder of Southern Sect of alchemical Daoism. He died in his hometown at the age of 96.

画中仙人据题签为北宋道士张伯端(984—1082)，道教内丹派南宗开山祖师。号紫阳道人，后世又称张紫阳。通儒释道三教经书。著有《悟真篇》一书。

Zhang Ziyang, by Yanhui, Yuan dynasty

画张紫阳　颜辉　元代

Chapter LXXIII

Brave and daring, one will be killed;

brave and not daring, one will survive.

Which of the two will do good or harm?

Who knows the reason

why heaven hates one or the other?

It is even difficult for the sage to

understand.

In accordance with heaven's divine law,

one may win without cotending,

respond without speaking,

come without being summoned.

and silent, one may plan well.

Heaven spreads a boundless net,

and none could escape escape through

its meshes.

dì qi shí sān zhāng
第 七 十 三 章

yǒng yú gǎn zé shā
勇 于 敢 则 杀；

yǒng yú bù gǎn zé huó
勇 于 不 敢 则 活。

cǐ liǎng zhě
此 两 者，

huò lì huò hài
或 利 或 害。

tiān zhi suǒ wù
天 之 所 恶，

shú zhi qí gù
孰 知 其 故？

shì yǐ shèng rén yóu nán zhi
是 以 圣 人 犹 难 之。

tiān zhi dào
天 之 道，

bù zhēng ér shàn shèng
不 争 而 善 胜，

bù yán ér shàn yìng
不 言 而 善 应，

bù zhào ér zì lái
不 召 而 自 来。

mò rán ér shàn móu
默 然 而 善 谋。

tiān wǎng huī huī
天 网 恢 恢，

shū ér bù shi
疏 而 不 失。

A Phoenix Tree Hut of One Hundred Square Feet, by an unknown author, Yuan dynasty

百尺梧桐轩图卷　无款　元代

It is a scenery of leisure household life. The host sitting in the exquisite that ched hall is Zhang Shixin, the third youngest brother of the prime minister, Zhang Shicheng (1321-1367). Zhang Shicheng was the head of the insurrectionary regime in south China, who proclaimed himself as the "King of Gusu" (now the city of Suzhou, Jiangsu). The attendant boy wearing long flowing air is serving tea for his master. There are a lot of phoenix trees, cherry bays and bamboos surrounding hut.

图绘园居闲适之景。中有一人便服闲坐于精雅的草顶轩堂中，此即张士诚的三弟张士信。左侧廊中一披发童子捧茗，草堂四周高桐环绕，间有桂树和竹林。画意是，赞美张士信广纳贤士之德性。

Chapter LXXIV

The people do not fear death.

Why threaten them with it?

If they ever fear it,

those who do evil

shall be caught and killed.

Who then would do evil again?

It is the executioner's duty to kill.

If you replace him,

it is like cutting wood in a carpenter's

place.

How can you not wound your hand?

dì qi shí sì zhāng
第 七 十 四 章

mín bù wèi sǐ
民 不 畏 死,

nài hé yǐ sǐ jù zhi
奈 何 以 死 惧 之?

ruò shǐ mín cháng wèi sǐ
若 使 民 常 畏 死,

ér wèi qí zhě
而 为 奇 者,

wǔ dé zhí ér shā zhi
吾 得 执 而 杀 之。

shú gǎn
孰 敢?

cháng yǒu si shā zhě shā
常 有 司 杀 者 杀。

fū dài si shā zhě shā
夫 代 司 杀 者 杀,

shì wèi dài dà jiàng zhuó
是 谓 代 大 匠 斫。

fū dài dà jiàng zhuó zhě
夫 代 大 匠 斫 者,

xi yǒu bù shāng qí shǒu yǐ
希 有 不 伤 其 手 矣。

The skyey peaks are shrouded in heavy snow, the several old tall trees are leafless and branchless, which enhances the desolateness. While the travelers resting under the pavilion and trees are carefree and comfortable. The clear hues of black and white produce a impressive effect.

此图绘雪峰突起，几棵参天的老树，枝疏叶稀，使画面增添了萧瑟的气氛。画面效果黑白分明，树下茅亭内行人停车小憩，安然自在。

The Snow, Pavilion and Resting Travelers, by Li Shida, Ming dynasty

雪亭小憩图　李士达　明代

Chapter LXXV

The people's starvation

results form the ruler' overtaxation,

so the people starve.

The people are difficult to rule,

for the ruler give exacting orders,

so the people are hard to rule.

The people make light of their death,

for the rulers overvalue their own life,

so the people undervalue their death.

Those who have no use for life

are better than those who value their life.

dì qī shí wǔ zhāng
第 七 十 五 章

mín zhī jī
民 之 饥,

yǐ qí shàng shí shuì zhī duō
以 其 上 食 税 之 多,

shì yǐ jī
是 以 饥。

mín zhī nán zhì
民 之 难 治,

yǐ qí shàng zhī yǒu wéi
以 其 上 之 有 为,

shì yǐ nán zhì
是 以 难 治。

mín zhī qīng sǐ
民 之 轻 死,

yǐ qí shàng qiú shēng zhī hòu
以 其 上 求 生 之 厚,

shì yǐ qīng sǐ
是 以 轻 死。

fū wéi wú yǐ shēng wéi zhě
夫 唯 无 以 生 为 者,

shì xián yú guì shēng
是 贤 于 贵 生。

Immortals on the Way Back from the Birthday Celebration, by Chou Ying, Ming dynasty

群仙会祝寿图（局部）　仇英　明代

The Eight Immortals are on their way back from the birthday party of Queen Mother of the West. They had a sea to cross. Lü Dongbin proposed that they should not mount on clouds, instead must cross the water with their own divine instruments, so that they could demonstrate their theurgies. Iron-crutch Li put his iron crutch onto water, Han Xiangzi his flower basket, Lü Dongbin his xiao(a vertical bamboo flute), Lan Caihe his clappers, Elder Zhang Guo his paper donkey, Royal Uncle Cao his jade tablet, Zhongli Han his drum and Immortal Lady He her bamboo hat.

本幅实即瑶池仙庆。群仙为西王母献寿。画中神仙相会，并有展现神通者，画意杂和八仙过海。八仙俱赴蟠桃大会，归途遇海，吕洞宾倡议不得乘云，各投物于水乘之以渡。于是李铁拐投仗，韩湘子投花篮，吕洞宾投箫管，蓝采和投拍板，张果老、曹国舅、汉钟离、何仙姑各显其能，各投以纸驴、玉版、鼓、竹罩，俱得渡。是谓八仙过海各显神通。

Chapter LXXVI

Man is born soft and weak；

dead, he becomes hard and stiff.

Grass and wood grow soft and supple；

dead, they become dry and withered.

So the hard and strong belong to death；

the soft and weak belong to life.

Therefore a strong army will be annihilated；

a sturdy tree will be cut down.

The soft and weak have the upper hand

of the hard and strong.

dì qī shí liù zhāng
第 七 十 六 章

rén zhī shēng
人 之 生

yě róu ruò
也 柔 弱，

qí sǐ yě jiān qiáng
其 死 也 坚 强。

wàn wù cǎo mù zhī shēng
万 物 草 木 之 生

yě róu cuì
也 柔 脆，

qí sǐ yě kū gǎo
其 死 也 枯 槁。

gù jiān qiáng zhě sǐ zhī tú
故 坚 强 者 死 之 徒，

róu ruò zhě shēng zhī tú
柔 弱 者 生 之 徒。

shì yǐ bīng qiáng zé bù shèng
是 以 兵 强 则 不 胜，

mù qiáng zé shé
木 强 则 折。

jiān qiáng chǔ xià
坚 强 处 下，

róu ruò chǔ shàng
柔 弱 处 上。

The snow-covered landscape is scattered with some dark green bamboos and trees. The old temple obscured by mist enhances a sense of transcendence. It is a quiet, peaceful and sublime world.

图绘雪后群山，银装素裹，山间乔木丛竹苍翠，烟岚笼罩下的古庙，倍觉神圣。全图营造出一个静谧、飘然的世界。

The Mountain and Brook on a Snowy Dusk, by an unknown author, Southern Song dynasty

溪山暮雪图　南宋

Chapter LXXVII

Is not the way of heaven's divine law

like the bending of a bow?

The high string shall be bent

and the bow shall be lifted.

We take from those who have enough and

to spare,

and give to those who have not enough.

In accordance with the divine law,

excess shall be reduced to supplement the

insufficient.

The human law is otherwise:

man takes from the poor to give to the

rich.

Who could give to the world more than

enough?

Only the follower of the divine law.

So the sage gives without being the giver,

and succeeds without being the successful,

for he will not be better than others.

dì qī shí qī zhāng
第 七 十 七 章

tiān zhī dào
天 之 道,

qí yóu zhāng gōng yú
其 犹 张 弓 欤?

gāo zhě yǎng zhī
高 者 抑 之,

xià zhě jǔ zhī
下 者 举 之;

yǒu yú zhě sǔn zhī
有 余 者 损 之,

bù zú zhě bǔ zhī
不 足 者 补 之。

tiān zhī dào
天 之 道,

sǔn yǒu yú ér bǔ bù zú
损 有 余 而 补 不 足;

rén zhī dào
人 之 道,

zé bù rán
则 不 然,

sǔn bù zú yǐ fèng yǒu yú
损 不 足 以 奉 有 余。

shú néng yǒu yú yǐ fèng tiān xià
孰 能 有 余 以 奉 天 下?

wéi yǒu dào zhě
唯 有 道 者。

shì yǐ shèng rén
是 以 圣 人

wéi ér bù shì
为 而 不 恃,

gōng chéng ér bù chù
功 成 而 不 处。

qí bù yù jiàn xiàn
其 不 欲 见 贤。

The Immortals Celebrating the Birthday of Queen Mother of the West, by an unknown author

图中所绘为诸神仙向天上王母祝寿的情形。

The Immortals Celebrating the Birthday of Queen Mother of the West, by an unknown author

群仙供寿

Chapter LXXVIII

Nothing in the world is softer and

weaker than water,

but nothing is better

to win over the hard and the strong,

for it cannot be replaced.

The weak may surpass the strong.

and the soft may surpass the hard.

It is well-known to the world,

but none can put it into practice.

That is the reason why the sage says:

"Who can bear the humiliation of a state

may become its master；

who can endure the diaster of a state

may become its ruler."

It seems wrong, but it is right.

dì qī shí bā zhāng
第 七 十 八 章

tiān xià mò róu ruò yú shuǐ
天 下 莫 柔 弱 于 水,

ér gōng jiān qiáng zhě
而 攻 坚 强 者

mò zhī néng shèng
莫 之 能 胜。

yǐ qí wú yǐ yì zhī yě
以 其 无 以 易 之 也。

ruò zhī shèng qiáng
弱 之 胜 强,

róu zhī shèng gāng
柔 之 胜 刚,

tiān xià mò bù zhī
天 下 莫 不 知,

mò néng xing
莫 能 行。

shì yǐ shèng rén yún
是 以 圣 人 云:

shòu guò zhī gòu
受 国 之 垢,

shì wèi shè jì zhǔ
是 谓 社 稷 主;

shòu guó zhī bù xiáng
受 国 之 不 祥,

shì wèi tiān xià wáng
是 为 天 下 王。

zhèng yán ruò fǎn
正 言 若 反。

The Poetry of Brook and Hut, by Dai Jin, Ming dynasty

溪堂诗意　戴进　明代

The right part of the picture is complicated and the left one is ethereal (somewhat empty). The peaks are high and steep, but the twin peaks in the middle look quite milk and round. The waterfall hanging between the peaks increases the lush and vital impression. The hut in the wood, the hermit on the chair and the visitor on the bridge echo each other. All the descriptions embody the word "serenity".

画面右侧繁复、左侧空灵。画中主峰高峻，中部双峰耸峙，极具委婉之态；两山间悬流瀑布，透露出空灵蓊郁的气象。近景茅庐深掩于茂树丛中，最近处访客行在小桥之上，与草庐中倚坐的士人构成呼应关系，处处体现了"幽"字。

Chapter LXXIX

Implacble hatred cannot be wholly
appeased.
Would it not be better
to return good for evil?
So the sage keeps the receipt
but never demands the payment.
A man of virtue keep the receipt;
a man without virtue exacts the payment.
The divine law is impartial,
but it always favors good men.

dì qì shí jiǔ zhāng
第 七 十 九 章

hé dà yuàn
和 大 怨,

bì yǒu yú yuàn
必 有 余 怨。

ān kě yǐ wéi shàn
安 可 以 为 善?

shì yǐ shèng rén zhī zuǒ qì
是 以 圣 人 执 左 契,

ér bù zé yú rén
而 不 责 于 人。

yǒu dé sī qì
有 德 司 契,

wú dé sī wěi
无 德 司 微。

tiān dào wú qīn
天 道 无 亲,

cháng yǔ shàn rén
常 与 善 人。

Zhong Kui is a figure of Chinese mythology. Traditionally regarded as a vanquisher of demons or King of the Ghost, his image is often painted on household gates as a guardian spirit. Zhong Kui's popularity in folklore can be traced to the reign of Emperor Xuanzong of Tang China. According to Song dynasty sources by Shen Kuo, once the Emperor Xuanzong was gravely ill. He had a dream in which he saw two ghosts. The smaller of the ghosts stole a purse from imperial consort Yang Guifei and a flute belonging to the emperor. The bigger ghost, wearing the hat of an official, captured the smaller ghost, tore out his eye and ate it. The ghost introduced himself as Zhong Kui. He said that he had sworn to rid the empire of evil. When the emperor awoke, he had recovered from his illness. So he commissioned the court painter Wu Daozi to produce an image of Zhong Kui to show to the officials. This was highly influential to later representations of Zhong.

据沈括《梦溪笔谈》记载：唐明皇梦见一大鬼捉一小鬼啖之，自称钟馗，生前应举不捷，死后成为鬼王，誓除天下恶鬼妖孽。明皇醒后乃命吴道子绘成图像。后来民间多悬其像以避鬼除邪。

Zhong Kui, by Ren Bonian, Qing dynasty

钟馗　任伯年　清代

Chapter LXXX

A small state with few people

may have hundreds of tools

but will not use them.

Its people value their life and death

and will not remove far away.

They may have boats and cars,

but they have no need to ride.

They may have armors and weapons,

but they have no need to use them.

They may return to the age of recording by

tying knots.

In an ideal state

people will find their food delicious,

their clothes beautiful,

their houses comfortable,

and their life delightful.

A neighboring state may be within sight,

with cocks' crow and dogs' bark within

hearing,

but people will not visit each other

till they die of old age.

dì bā shí zhāng
第 八 十 章

xiǎo guó guǎ mín
小 国 寡 民。

shǐ yǒu shí mò zhī qì
使 有 阡 陌 之 器,

ér bù yòng
而 不 用。

shǐ mín zhòng sǐ
使 民 重 死,

ér bù yuǎn xǐ
而 不 远 徙。

suī yǒu zhōu yú
虽 有 舟 舆,

wú suǒ chéng zhī
无 所 乘 之。

suī yǒu jiǎ bīng
虽 有 甲 兵,

wú suǒ chén zhī
无 所 陈 之。

shǐ mín fù jié shéng ér yòng zhī
使 民 复 结 绳 而 用 之。

gān qí shí
甘 其 食,

měi qí fú
美 其 服,

ān qí jā
安 其 居,

lè qí sú
乐 其 俗。

lín guó xiāng wàng
邻 国 相 望,

ji quǎn zhī shēng xiāng wén
鸡 犬 之 声 相 闻,

mín zhì lǎo sǐ
民 至 老 死

bù xiāng wǎng lái
不 相 往 来。

Mount Wudang is a Daoist Sacred
Mountain. The sky is clearing up after
snow, the temple, mountain and trees
are more clean, quite and mysterious.

武当山是著名的道教名山，本幅
描绘层峦叠翠的武当山道观，在
融融白雪的映衬下，显得格外道
气盎然。

The Sceneries After Snow at Purple Sky Palace on Mount Wudang, by
Xie Shichen, Ming dynasty

武当山紫霄宫霁雪　谢士臣　明代

183

Chapter LXXXI

Truthful words may not be beautiful;
beautiful words may not be truthful.
A good man need not justify himself;
who justifies himself may not be a good
man.
A wise man may not be learned;
a learned man may not be wise.
A sage does not keep things for himself.
The more he helps others, the more he still
has.
The more he gives, the more he keeps.
The divine law
will do all good and no harm.
The way of a sage
is to do what he can but contend with
none.

dì bā shí yī zhāng
第 八 十 一 章

xìn yán bù měi
信 言 不 美,

měi yán bù xìn
美 言 不 信。

shàn zhě bù biàn
善 者 不 辩,

biàn zhě bù shàn
辩 者 不 善。

zhī zhě bù bó
知 者 不 博,

bó zhě bù zhī
博 者 不 知。

shèng rén bù jī
圣 人 不 积,

jì yǐ wéi rén jǐ yù yǒu
既 以 为 人 己 愈 有,

jì yǐ yǔ rén jǐ yù duō
既 以 与 人 己 愈 多。

tiān zhī dào lì ér bù hài
天 之 道 利 而 不 害。

shèng rén zhī dào wèi ér bù zhēng
圣 人 之 道 为 而 不 争。

This picture presents the learning journey of Yellow Emperor to Guangchengzi in Mount Kongdong. The emperor dressed in dragon robe is mounting along the steep path to deep gully. The old pines symbolize the everlasting vitalities of Dao, the emperor's identity the precious value, the very craggy cliffs and unfrequented track remind people of hardship of access to Dao.

此图描绘轩辕黄帝至崆峒山向广成子问道的故事。画面左侧峰峦突起，直入云宵，右侧古松茂蔚，老干虬枝，山谷险道上，身着衮服的黄帝孤身赴洞天问道。

The Yellow Emperor's Journey to Requesting Dao,
by Dai Jin, Ming dynasty

洞天问道图　戴进　明代

图书在版编目(CIP)数据

道德经与神仙画／五洲传播出版社编
—北京：五洲传播出版社　2006.1
ISBN 7-5085-0846-7

Ⅰ．道... Ⅱ．①五... ②许... ③曾...
Ⅲ．①道家 ②老子－哲学思想－汉、英
Ⅳ．B223.11

中国版本图书馆(CIP)数据核字(2005)第 116863 号

经文翻译：许渊冲
辅文翻译：曾传辉
图片编辑：蔡　程
　　　　　任正炜
特约审稿：王宜峨

道德经与神仙画

出版发行：五洲传播出版社

策划编辑：荆孝敏　　　　　　**责任编辑：刘　涛／荆孝敏**
装帧设计：任正炜／屈银菊／谢　倩

社址：北京市海淀区北小马厂 6 号　　　邮政编码：100038
发行电话：010-58891281　　　　　　传真：58891281
网址：www.cicc.org.cn

制版单位：北京紫航文化艺术有限公司
印刷：北京市华审彩色印刷厂
开本：720×980　1/16　　印张：12

2006 年 1 月
ISBN 7-5085-0846-7/B·62　　　　　　定价：78.00 元